Clare

**The Incredible Story
of a
Western Australian Built Wooden Ketch**

Nigel Ridgway
with
Aileen Ridgway and Lanie Verboon

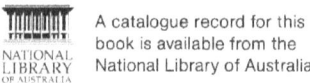
A catalogue record for this book is available from the National Library of Australia

Copyright © 2022 Nigel Ridgway
All rights reserved.
ISBN-13: 9781-922727-13-8

Linellen Press
265 Boomerang Road
Oldbury, Western Australia
www. linellenpress. com. au

Dedication

Dedicated to all sailors of wooden boats – past and present – who have ventured offshore into the world's oceans. It is you who have solved many of the mysteries of Planet Earth during your explorations.

Contents

Dedication iii
Contents v
Acknowledgments vii
Foreword by John Longley 1
Preface 3
Chapter One - Sailing to Cocos (Keeling) 5
Chapter Two - Staying at Cocos & Some of its History 24
Chapter Three - Clare's History 42
    That damn plank! 62
    Clare in the News 63
Chapter Four - Lanie's Story 67
Chapter Five - Lanie's Story from Melbourne to the Whitsundays 79
Chapter Six - Wooden boat building in WA 94
Chapter Seven - Brad's Story and Clare Today 106
    Here's Brad's story: 106
Epilogue 114
Great Sailing Reads! 115
About the Author 117

Acknowledgments

Many thanks to my wife, Aileen, who helped with the editing and for her contribution to the story.

Thanks also to Lanie and Brad who had to put up with my emailing!

And a thank you to Helen at Linellen Press for accepting my manuscript and for encouraging me to keep writing.

Foreword

by John Longley

I have had two particularly memorable days in my long sailing journey. The first as a crewman on *Australia II* as she crossed the line on 26th September 1983 to be the first yacht to wrest the America's Cup from the Americans. The second standing on the launching platform on the 9th December 1993 watching *Endeavour* charge down the slips into Fremantle Fishing Boat Harbour.

That journey, which continues today albeit on a lesser scale, started when, as a fourteen-year-old Naval Sea Cadet, I learnt to sail in a 27-foot clinker-built wooden Navy Whaler. Although my journey has seen me sailing on boats of most types of construction – fibreglass, aluminium, carbon fibre – it is the timber vessels that I have been involved with that hold a special interest and fascination.

In this delightful book, based on the life of a simple small timber ketch, the reader gets an understanding of the way timber yachts can work their way into your soul.

Anybody who 'knows boats' also knows that a timber boat, particularly an old one, is a recipe for tears of anguish as a new piece of rot or broken rib is discovered, and tears of pain as another cheque is written to keep the boat going! And yet people still take them on, usually as a 'project' with misty-eyed dreams of rolling down the Trades with an organic living boat that you deeply love.

How do so many of these boats survive for so long?

Why do normally sensible people dive in and work and fund the restoration of often very tired wooden boats?

This book does not answer those questions because they are unanswerable, but it does give a hint as to what an answer might look like. It will also help feed those misty eyes as one reads of the delightful yarns and adventures that inevitably flow from throwing off the dock lines for a deep-sea voyage.

I hope you enjoy the story of *Clare,* who has survived for 70 years and, hopefully, will do so for many more.

John Longley AM CitWA

Preface

What is it about a wooden sailing vessel? They capture hearts in a way that other building materials do not. You may think you own a wooden boat – but I'm sure, after owing two of them – that they own you! We owned four 'plastic' (fibreglass) yachts before *Clare* but the minute my wife and I stepped aboard our 12m (40 foot) ketch – we were hooked. There was just an intangible presence as we made our way below to the warmth of her saloon – the gleaming varnish, the exposed beams and the feeling of security. We had to have her.

Well, owning Clare took us on a fascinating journey, both historically and on the ocean, but they were probably the best (and most expensive) years we had owning a yacht.

Wooden boat building has always been a part of WA's history and continues today in a small way. Jarrah is such a wonderful timber – very strong, its resins reject teredo worm (the curse of wooden vessels in the past); its durability and beauty are enduring. You will discover the beauty of jarrah in the pages of this book – the timbers that went into the building of *Clare* are pristine, even after 70 years.

We can all recall the momentous occasions of the launching of the *Endeavour* in Fremantle, then later the equally exciting moment of the *Duyfken's* birth and launch. Both vessels are a tribute to WA's shipbuilding and wooden boat shipwrights, skills which we have in Western Australia and are the envy of the world. Both vessels now lie in Sydney, at the Sydney Maritime Museum; both ships sail on the harbour and bring joy and wonder to countless people, both young and old.

Clare may not be as famous, but she has a really interesting history. Unlike the *Endeavour* and *Duyfken*, *Clare* was constructed entirely of WA timber back in 1951. She, too, lies in the eastern states, at Hastings in Victoria. The seven years we owned her, from 1991 to 1998, were a huge learning curve – like a jealous mistress, she consumed lots of our time and money. There is nothing like the creaks and groans of a wooden boat in a seaway, always reminding you of the importance of the sailing ship to the world's history, trade, exploration (and exploitation) and commerce. We loved *Clare*, and it's been a real pleasure researching her story, telling her sailing adventures, her highs and lows (a timber boat can be a heartbreaker) and rejoicing in the knowledge that her current owner, Brad, has the perfect skill set to prolong the life of this fine ketch.

Chapter One

Sailing to Cocos (Keeling)

'Sailing – it leaves you speechless, then turns you into a storyteller,"

Ibn Buttuta

I was on watch, Aileen and John down below sleeping. I was sitting in the cockpit listening to the wind and seas as they eased off. Trade winds do often ease off in the night. I climbed out of the cockpit and made my way aft to sit on top of the little aft cabin – I could hear John's gentle snoring below. I sat there entranced, listening to the gurgle under her counter as she ambled along at about five knots. A happy ship! Then the first glimpse of the moon popped up on the horizon, seemingly right behind us. It gradually rose until it was a full moon, shimmering on the swells. A beautiful sight, and I felt at peace with the world, just a gentle roll from the ship and the swish of the seas.

Here we were at sea, many miles out into the Indian Ocean sailing along in our 12m (40-foot) wooden ketch *Clare*, heading to Cocos (Keeling) in the tropics. The night was warm, the breeze about 12 knots and our sails were poled out to catch it. It was one of the times when you feel completely alive, at one with nature and part of the cycle of life on Planet Earth. I had a feeling of peace and relief that all the years of preparation had paid off and that we were actually *doing it!* We really were sailing our traditional timber ketch across the ocean. I thought of all the time and expense that had gone into the project – you can't just jump on your boat and go – and I felt that it had all been worthwhile to experience this lovely trade wind sailing.

Then I remembered a dream I'd had not long before we left Geraldton. It was so vivid. A gnarled, wizened hand clutched my forearm and an old, but strong, voice warned, "Don't go!" I awoke immediately and couldn't get back to sleep, the warning had been so clear. But I shook off that feeling of dread – the weather forecast was reasonable, the rellies were coming to see us off, and a daily radio sked had been arranged with the year 7 kids back at my school. I guess we felt under some pressure to go, so I dismissed the warning. Sitting on the aft cabin, all seemed okay, so I again put that dream out of my mind and concentrated on enjoying *Clare's* gentle motion as we gradually fetched Cocos.

At the end of my two-hour watch, I tapped on the cabin top to wake John. We shared a few swigs of scotch and a cuppa, and then I turned in, trying hard not to wake my wife, Aileen.

****

How did we end up out there on the ocean? Like all dreamers, I had read many, many ocean sailing stories and had loved authors like Bernard Moitessier, Robin Knox-Johnson, Joshua Slocum, John Wray, Francis Chichester, Lin and Larry Pardey and Kay Cottee, plus many others and it drove me to try it for myself. In 1990, I sailed a little 29ft sloop, *Lotus II*, to South Africa and back to Fremantle, visiting the Mascarine Islands of Rodrigues, Mauritius, and La Reunion, as well as Cocos (Keeling). I described the voyage in a book titled, *Lotus II – an Indian Ocean Adventure* (1992), which led to me becoming the WA correspondent for *Cruising Helmsman* magazine for about twenty years. I loved *Lotus II* but she was a bit small for my wife Aileen and I to live on for ocean sailing, so we dreamt of owning a bigger yacht with a centre cockpit for protection from the elements.

WARNING! Do not harbour these thoughts – they will lead you into more expense and lots of work!

One day we were wandering along the jetty at Sorrento Quay, Hillarys Boat Harbour, just looking at the yachts for sale tied up in the pens there, when we spotted this timber ketch. She looked huge after little *Lotus* so we plucked up courage, entered the yacht broker's office and enquired about her. The broker seemed very pleased to have someone show some interest in the boat, so he just gave us the keys and said, "Go and have a look!"

Well, that did it!

Opening up the companionway hatch, we climbed down some fairly steep steps into an oldie world of wonder.

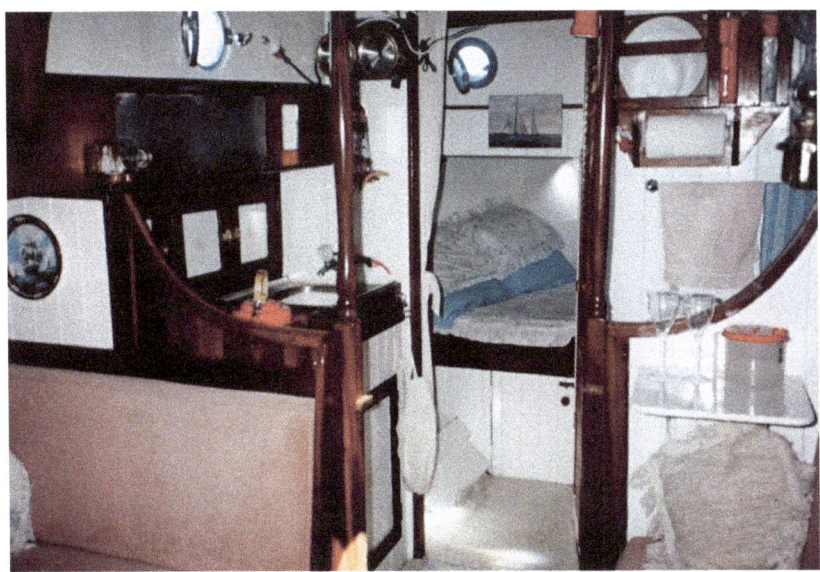

Classic wooden interior – very warm and cosy below!

Beautiful varnish everywhere, exposed beams and pink champagne coloured seat cushions – and the space! We fell in love almost immediately and had to have her. We forgot the golden rule – don't buy in haste – but we did. Out on deck, we loved the wide side decks and solid feel, and she also had that sought after centre cockpit.

Centre covered cockpit /doghouse – we had to have her!

There really is something intangible about wooden boats. They evoke so many feelings that I think are deep in our genes – after all, it is the sailing ships of the past that opened up the world's trading routes and brought so many immigrants to different countries around the world. We all have sailors, explorers or early settlers genes in our family histories.

So that was it. *Lotus II* sold very quickly (Duncanson 29s are very popular) and we were now the proud owners of *Clare,* a forty-foot wooden ketch. Once we had moved her into our pen in the public marina, we set about researching her history and came across some surprises. She was not what the broker had purported her to be.

Some stats of *Clare* are: 12.4m length, 3.6m beam, 1.8m draft and built from 38mm (one and a half inch) jarrah. Her builder was listed by the broker as the well-known Arthur Bishop, her designer, Maurice Griffiths of the UK (circa 1963). Arthur has built some lovely wooden boats in Perth and Fremantle, but *Clare* was not one of his.

The broker had spun us a yarn to help sell the boat. We didn't do much about that at first but, after our initial sail to Rottnest, we changed our minds. As we approached Thomson's Bay and started the engine, we found we had no forward drive. We found a sandy patch and quickly dropped the anchor, which luckily held. I opened up the engine room doors and checked the gearbox fluid – it was empty. There were a couple of tins of transmission fluid (ATF) in the engine room, so I topped up the gearbox and we had drive. All was okay until our second sail, and that was to the Mindarie Marina and back to Hillarys. Well, the same thing happened again – no forward drive, and we were very close to reef near Hillarys. We could not do short tacks with the big boat, so I called up Marine and Harbours to tow us in. I was furious. The broker had not mentioned that the front seal of the gearbox had a leak, causing the fluid to drain out.

Clare working to windward off the WA coast

We managed to sail *Clare* down to Fremantle where a diesel mechanic pulled the gearbox off and replaced the seal. We never had any more problems with the drive after that. However, we were still very angry that the broker hadn't let us know about the leak (that's obviously why the tins of automatic transmission fluid were in the engine room). The broker just shrugged it off but we were very concerned as it had been a safety issue. We then made contact with Arthur Bishop himself, and he told us that he had nothing to do with *Clare*. That really got us going, and we filed a complaint with the Small Claims Tribunal, accusing the broker of misrepresentation.

The day of the hearing was extraordinary. We sat and waited for the magistrate to arrive, then the broker came in. He walked straight up to the bench and put out his hand to the magistrate. The broker said, "Don't I know you?"

"Sit down!" the magistrate ordered, "and be quiet."

We presented our case about the false claim of the builder and also mentioned the gearbox leak. The broker protested loudly, interrupting the magistrate. After some deliberation, the magistrate brought down his decision. We won the case and were awarded $5,000 compensation. The broker (who shall be nameless but is a well-known figure among boating circles in Perth) got into the lift with us after the hearing and proceeded to tell us that he was 'going to get us'. That was a bit scary as he is a big bloke and very wealthy. Fortunately, it was all bluff, and we never heard from him again.

****

Chart of the Indian Ocean

Anyway, let's go back to sea and enjoy the voyage.

After sailing *Clare* for seven years in local offshore waters, our trip to Cocos was planned. We worked out an itinerary to visit some of our Indian Ocean islands: Cocos (Keeling), the Maldives, The Chagos Archipelago, Mauritius and La Reunion. From Reunion, we would work our way south until we caught the westerlies to drive us home to Fremantle. A few years of preparation preceded this adventure, which I describe a bit later.

We left Hillarys on 19th April 1998 with sailing friends John and Julie Rees as crew. Aileen and John's wife, Julie, sailed with us as far as Two Rocks – Aileen then went home to sort out things before finishing work. She would meet us in Geraldton. Another sailing friend, John Leslie, joined us as third hand at Two Rocks and the girls drove his car back to Perth. We had a leisurely cruise up the coast, calling in at the fishing ports of Lancelin, Jurien Bay and Dongara (Port Denison), fetching Geraldton on 23rd April. We three boys had a great time, and *Clare* romped along in the fresh breezes.

Casting off mooring lines at Hillarys Yacht Club

We planned an early May departure for Cocos. That gave us time to sort out any hassles, to stock up on supplies and buy any extra equipment needed. The list seemed to get longer and longer! By the 2nd of May, we were ready and some of the family and a few friends drove up from Perth to wave us goodbye. It's always a bit emotional saying goodbye to sailors, and I guess it's been that way since time immemorial. We started the engine and made our way out of the Geraldton small boat harbour; Aileen at the helm, John and I tidying up the mooring lines and fenders. After some tears, it was time to settle down and set watches. The bureau of meteorology had given us a moderately good forecast.

The first day was nice and easy with a light W/SW breeze and slight seas. We spotted a pod of Minke whales nearby. We were enthralled as they breached beside *Clare*, throwing up great mountains of spray before they splashed back into the depths again. They showed little interest in us. It was cold corned beef and vegies for dinner that night.

About 0200 the next morning, the wind shifted to the North West and rose to about 15kts, then gusting to 35kts. We hove-to (stopped the boat by heading up into the seas with the rudder opposing the reefed mainsail). It rained! Not a very pleasant start to the voyage.

Day three was awful – thunderstorms, lightning and a rising sea. We stayed hove-to, *Clare* just fore-reaching a bit, shouldering the seas well. She felt solid and very safe.

Big following seas

Aileen became seasick, although she never normally suffers, and stayed below in our bunk. I think it was fear of the unknown, rather than the motion, that caused it. John and I kept watch, taking an occasional swig on our duty-free scotch to keep us going through the night. Our bright masthead light lit up the angry seas, and we would have been easy to spot by a passing ship.

Eventually, the gale blew out, but not before I had fed a few fish too. John was marvellous and has a cast-iron stomach. He never gets seasick. With the wind shifting round to the south, we began to make good progress with daily runs of over 100 nautical miles. A fairly large swell persisted right behind us, causing a good roll but we gradually became used to the motion. That swell followed us all the way to Cocos, a distance of 1,400 nm (or 2,592 kms).

On Day four, a new high-pressure system in the Bight caused strong winds to blow across the north of Australia, far out into the Indian Ocean, and it got to us north of the latitude of North West Cape. This one was really strong. The wind howled in at 40 knots from the east, gusting even higher. John and I doused the main, tucked two rolls into the furling staysail and went for it. Huge seas, big swells had *Clare* screaming along at 9 knots under this tiny sail area. We opened the second bottle of duty-free. Things improved immensely after that.

Aileen's log extract, Day 4:

> *Day 4 – Sailed out of the low (shit weather) into a ridge of high pressure – very strong winds gusting to 45kts – huge seas and swell, at times up to 8 meters. John steered all night, said he was grateful of the dark so he couldn't see the huge seas behind! 'Clare' was handling the conditions marvellously. South West-South winds. Our course was set again for 315 degrees. During the bad weather we sometimes had to run with the wind and squalls and not always in the right direction for Cocos. We had been in*

touch with Perth Radio and the yachts Manyana and Sorcerer – giving them our position daily and sometimes twice a day. I have never been so frightened as on that night of Day 4.

As we sailed up into the tropics, the weather became warmer and the trade winds started to kick in. Life became pleasant. Aileen recovered from her bout of *mal de mer* and got stuck into the galley, producing some delicious meals. We all began to relax and laugh and enjoy the ride. We called up Telstra on the HF radio and they patched us through to my school, Joondalup Primary. The year 7 teachers had organised the students to create a large chart to follow our progress. The kids were excited to talk to us on the high seas.

*Joondalup Primary School Year 7s –
my radio sked students who tracked the voyage*

We gave them our position, our daily runs (distance sailed) and they asked if we'd seen any sea or birdlife. We told them about the minke whales and some dolphins we'd seen and about the stormy petrels and other seabirds flying around *Clare*. We also mentioned the flying fish that flew up and landed on the deck every night. One actually flew into the cockpit and hit me on the back of the head – a great shock! It was really great talking to the kids, but John had to take over once when I got squeamish and had to rush up top to chuck over the side. The kids loved that bit!

Back at school, all the information was assembled on that huge chart and was of great interest to the staff, kids and parents. I think it was one of the more worthwhile things I did as a teacher at that school. It gave us a kick on board too, and we always looked forward to the daily sked (only during the week, of course, there being no hook-up on the weekends). Telstra was very good about it all, and I don't recall there being any cost for the calls. Calls at sea can be very expensive, especially through HF (High Frequency) and VHF (Very High Frequency) radios. Of course, these days, a sailor would have a Satellite Phone, which is so easy to use – just dial the number and you're through.

John is a keen fisherman and he had this large reel attached to the stern rail. The line was pretty thick and his stainless steel traces were really strong. As the weather improved, he attached a lure and let out a long line for trolling. It was not long before the reel started going mad as a fish grabbed the lure and raced off! John applied the reel brake and we slowed *Clare* down to haul in our catch. As the fish got closer, we could see vibrant colours of gold, greens and blues pulsating through its terrified body as it tried to shake off the lure. We brought him up to the transom and hauled him on board. It was a dorado (dolphin fish or mahi-mahi) a pelagic hunter and about one and a half metres long. On board, he turned grey as if he knew it was his end. John had to expedite his demise to stop him thrashing about. I helped hold him down but am a bit squeamish about killing things, so looked away.

A big dorado (mahi-mahi or dolphin fish). Great eating!

His stomach was full of flying fish but that didn't really surprise us, as flying fish glide for ages to get away from these pelagic hunters, but it's not that obvious, as the drama occurs beneath the waves. We cut lots of steaks off and had enough fish to last the three of us for three days for dinner. They are delicious eating but quite rich if you overdo it. We caught another one of similar size a few days later. We only took what was needed for food and not just for the sport.

With three crew on *Clare,* it was much easier to set watches and do all the little chores on board. It meant that we could all have a reasonable sleep. Once in the trades, we could douse the main and mizzen completely and just sail under the 'twins.' This was something I'd read about in sailing stories and was dying to try. We poled out the staysail and yankee (the jib set on the bowsprit) – one on each side of the boat, and it was a pretty sight to watch the sails drawing and pulling us along nicely.

Trade wind sailing under 'the twins'

We rolled a fair bit so we did have to hang on when moving about. An incident that was probably a bit foolish in hindsight was when the mainsail halyard came adrift from the top of the sail. It was hanging right out in front of the boat, right up in the air well beyond reach. John taped two boathooks together and climbed up on the pulpit rail, one hand on the forestay, balancing there as the ship rolled downwind. Bloody stupid really, as one slip and he'd have gone overboard and it would have taken Aileen and me a long time to get the sails down, turn the engine on and get back to him in the ocean. Aileen was down below and missed the drama but we would have been well and truly dressed down by her if she saw John precariously perched out on the pulpit! A lull in the breeze enabled him to grab the halyard eventually.

Aileen's Log extract, Day 7:

Day 7 – Daily run 120 miles – Winds S-SW in the morning up to 20knots turning to SE in the afternoon and freshening. Course still 310-316deg really good sailing but big swells still. Sometimes 'Clare' surfs down the face of them.

Cooked vegetable and beef stew for tea – was excellent. The days seem to be rushing by now and soon it is night time again. I am becoming a little more relaxed with the night times now. The boys do the washing up in salt water in buckets after the main meal. We are only having two meals a day – late breakfast and early tea. I start to prepare tea at about 4pm. It gets dark really early about 6.30pm. All our meals are eaten out in the cockpit.

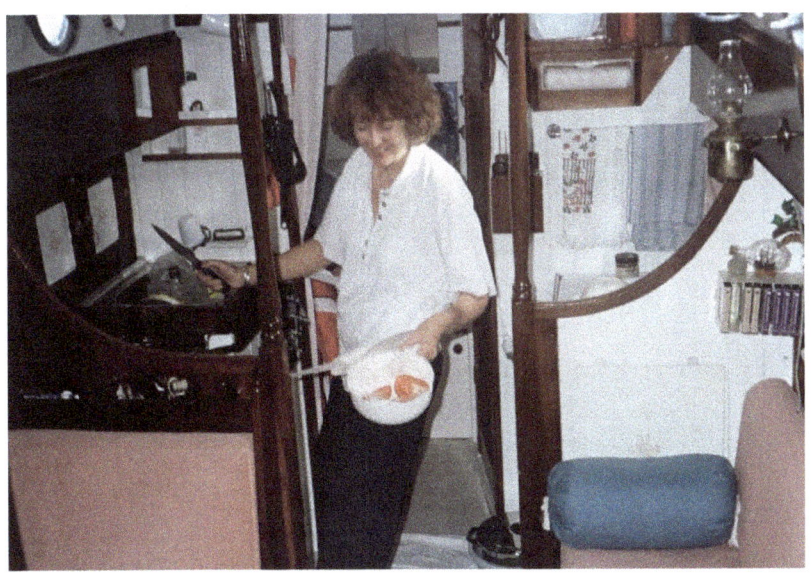

Aileen in the galley at sea – waist strap to prevent falling

Round about day ten, I awoke to hear a thump with each roll of the boat. It seemed to be coming from the engine room. We lifted the doors open and I climbed down for a look. One battery bank had come partly adrift and was thumping onto the side of the boat each time we rolled. I had to lash the bank down with ropes and luckily it gave us no more trouble. That was really the only thing that gave us any hassles. All other systems on *Clare* worked well and I was very proud of our timber vessel. She was heavy and strong and quite comfortable in the seas and swell.

The boys wash up on the high seas!

Something that gave us a real laugh one morning was when we were all sitting out in the cockpit enjoying breakfast. John loves his bread and his last Geraldton loaf came out and he began to chew on the end it, just as a bigger wave smacked into the side of the boat and jumped into the cockpit. John's bread was soaked but he still ate it salt water flavoured!

With the warmer weather we could take turns having a shower on the foredeck, using a solar-bag to warm up the fresh water. Our daily runs were improving with the best being 150nm under the twin headsails. Life at sea is quite enjoyable when the weather is kind but you still have to take care moving about and it takes time to get used to the rolling, pitching and heaving motion of a yacht at sea. And, yes, you do get the creaks and groans of the timbers as she makes her way through the seas (just like you hear in those old sailing movies!)

Aileen's Log extract, Day 11:

> Day 11 – Daily run 130NM, course 350deg. Changed sail set to broad reach, Yankee and one reef in the main. Light winds, SE 12knots. 450 NM to Cocos! Magic sailing. Deck showers and hair wash, even put some curlers in my hair! Veg and pasta one pot meal with left over fish for tea – sliced pineapple for sweets. Last two days have eaten too many lollies e. g. jubes, licorice etc. Afternoon swell rolled in again, uncomfortable, the wind piped up. Very uncomfortable night. I only got about 3 hours sleep hence a bit grumpy. Ran engine to boost batteries and cool the fridge. Fridge not very successful. I am really missing not having chilled food and drinks. Air temperature is about 30degC and it is very humid".

By the 13th day, Cocos was dead ahead and the trades blowing a steady 15 – 25 knots. That night the weather deteriorated again. Down came the rain and we knew we just could not make landfall before dark. We hove-to all night. Through the gloom, we could just make out the aircraft strobe light on West Island. The phosphorescence surrounding us was awesome – it was as if the ocean was on fire underneath and all round *Clare*. (Tiny marine organisms cause phosphorescence, as a sort of flight mechanism – the scientific name is *Noctiluca Milaris*, it being more prevalent in tropical waters). By this time we were on our third bottle of duty free and Aileen was swigging on the bottle like the rest of the motley crew. It warms the cockles of 'yer 'eart – as old salts say.

Early next morning, we motored round the end of Direction Island, picking out the markers to get into Port Refuge. *Clare's* motion ceased in the still waters of the lagoon – marvellous. We were fourteen days from Geraldton, pretty slow but then we hadn't anticipated being hove-to for two nights. The lagoon still looked gorgeous, even though it was blowing half a gale and raining. We dropped the pick near the quarantine buoy and called up Customs on VHF Ch. 20.

Clare at anchor, Direction Island, Cocos (Keeling)

****

There I was back at Cocos after eight years previously in *Lotus II*. It all looked pretty much the same – there were the coconut palms, there was the lean-to shelter and table on Direction Island (DI), there was the water tank for yachties and below us, the turquoise-blue waters of this idyllic anchorage. The only new constructions I could see were an ablution block and a Telstra phone booth.

Dieter, the customs/quarantine officer was soon alongside to clear us in. He was full of apologies for another change. During 1998, a charge of $A105 for clearance had been introduced and I think we were the first yacht to cop it. It was double that if you arrived on the weekend. It was all free back in 1990.

Had these pristine atolls changed much in eight years? Once we'd cleared in and moved closer to DI, an immediate change we noted was that there was no longer a free ferry service between Direction Island and Home Island. It was now going to necessitate a ride in the rubber ducky, a distance of about 1nm. From Home Island, the free ferry to West Island was still operating. On Home Island, I noticed a couple of new little shops and observed that the Coco-Malays seemed much more open and relaxed with visitors.

John's wife, Julie, flew in on the weekly charter from Perth and spent a couple of weeks with us on *Clare*. The first week the weather was dreadful – tropical lows with lots of wind and rain which the weather bureau on West Island put down to El Nino – that little boy has a lot to answer for. However, the second week was much better as things cleared up and we enjoyed some tropical sunshine and lighter winds, which is what we'd come for.

Chapter Two

Staying at Cocos & Some of its History

"Islands are matured workshops of evolution,"
David Wolfe

The Cocos (Keeling) group of islands comprise North Keeling, which is an uninhabited bird-sanctuary and South Keeling, which consists of 27 coral atolls. The islands lie about 12 degrees south of the equator and 96 degrees east, in the tropics. The climate is very humid but the maximum temperature seldom exceeds 30 degrees - mainly because they are in the trade-wind belt. The only inhabited islands of South Keeling are West Island and Home Island. The islands are an Australian Government Territory and the population (census 2016) is 544 – 140 on West Island and 404 on Home Island. In 1990, the total population was about 730. Ex-pats live on West Island (mostly public servants) and the Coco-Malay community resides on Home Island. They practice a Muslim lifestyle and the different culture is quite fascinating. The islands have an interesting history.

The coral atolls were first discovered (as far as we know) by Captain Keeling in 1608 whilst he was employed by the VOC, or Dutch East India Company. Nothing was done with them for years, probably because of the lack of spices and minerals, until Captain John Clunies-Ross clapped eyes on them in 1814. He vowed to claim them and this he did two years later, arriving with his family and eight tough sailors. Unfortunately, he found an eccentric, wealthy Englishman there already – a strange bloke called Alexander Hare. Hare had planned to live out his days in the tropical paradise and accordingly, had brought along a concubine of Malay women with him to enjoy his solitude. Sparks were bound to fly between the rival colonists, and they did. Hare and his harem were no match for eight lusty sailors and eventually the women joined the Clunies-Ross's group. Poor Hare was not impressed and ended up being driven away. He ended his days in Batavia (now Jakarta) and, from all accounts, went mad.

But Captain Clunies-Ross went from strength to strength. He established coconut plantations and a thriving copra industry that was quite viable until synthetic oils took over and were cheaper to produce. Ross became the founder of a dynasty that stretches until today. The Clunies-Ross family became the 'Kings of Cocos' and their subjects were the Malays who interbred with the sailors to become Coco-Malays.

The wily old captain claimed the islands for the British but retained, in effect, control of the atolls. He claimed Queen Victoria bequeathed them to him. They remained part of the British Empire until 1955 when they became an Australian Territory. The family continued to 'rule' Cocos until 1973, when a snooping reporter told the story to an amazed Australian population. At that time, the Coco-Malays were virtual slaves living in a feudal system. They were 'paid' in tokens that could only be redeemed in the shop, which was owned by Clunies-Ross! We can only imagine the field day the media had. The ensuing furore caused the Australian Government heaps of embarrassment and questions about human rights were even brought up at the United Nations.

Eventually the Coco-Malays were granted independence but after a referendum, elected to remain part of Australia. Clunies-Ross received some compensation from the government which he invested in a Singaporean shipping company. Rumour has it that the company went broke and he lost the lot.

The Grand House, the former stately home of the family, fell into disrepair for many years but has now been turned into accommodation for tourists. The final 'heir' to the throne, John Clunies-Ross, still lives at Cocos but has moved to West Island. He's involved in a dive company and fish farming. He's a really nice guy and we had a wonderful Sunday lunch with him and other ex-pats in 1990, after we'd anchored there in *Lotus II*. It was served up on a huge 'King Arthur'-like round table and we had an entertaining afternoon swapping stories. John has accepted that the dynasty had to end, as it really was an anachronism in the 20th century.

For many years the islands were an important link for the British Overseas Telegraph Company and a telegraphic post was established on Direction Island. This was of some strategic importance in both world wars. The Japanese tried to silence the outpost by shelling it in WWII but due to clever deception, the equipment remained intact.

One of the few blots on Australian Naval history occurred in World War I with the sinking of the German cruiser, *Emden*. The *Emden* had been harassing and sinking allied shipping in the Indian Ocean and orders went out to sink her. She called in at Cocos to capture the telegraph station on DI but was caught out during the operation by *HMAS Sydney (1)*. The *Emden* was engaged and put out of action, the German captain deciding to beach her on North Keeling. The story goes that the *Sydney* continued to shell the stricken ship, even after the white surrender flag was raised. Not very sportsman-like of the Aussies.

Some of the Germans left behind on DI stole the Clunies-Ross schooner *Ayesha* and sailed her to Indonesia where they, sadly, eventually scuttled her before boarding a Dutch freighter. How they got themselves back to Germany through the Red Sea and Arabia is one of the most amazing escape stories of the Great War. They were hailed as heroes back in Germany but of course, due to propaganda, their incredible exploits were never reported in Britain or Australia.

It was fun musing on all this as we sat comfortably at anchor on *Clare*.

After washing all the salt off us over on DI under the shower there, we gathered up our washing to take to West Island to launder. The first part of the journey was in our dinghy to Home Island and then we caught the ferry to West Island.

Aileen takes up the story of our stay at the atolls from her journal:

> *Our trip to West Island was good and we asked a Telstra worker to give us a lift to the settlement in his ute. He dropped our things off at the Lodge and took us to the Post Office to see if there was any mail for us. There was! Great joy – letters from Mum, Suzanne, Dennis and Mary and Samantha. We bought post cards to send home and stamps etc.*
>
> *Our room, number 19, was ok. At least it had 240 volt electricity, hot water and a fridge. Number 19 is on the edge of the water, literally, and because of the land breezes and huge sea swells the surf was breaking about 25 metres out in the most incredible way. Huge dumpers were crashing on the beach, making a blasting-like noise, almost too loud to sleep. We ate at the Lodge restaurant for lunch and in the evening went to the Cocos Club across the road. Cheap cold drinks with ice and a sausage sizzle. Chatted to a few Aussies working on Cocos and watched hermit crab races. People not that friendly but we felt comfortable. The Air Force was laid over because of electrical problems with their Orion plane. Good bunch.*
>
> *Saturday 23rd May, Julie arrives today. John arrived at*

West Island Lodge about 1pm. They have room number 17. We hung about at the Lodge and Club waiting for Julie's plane to arrive which it eventually did, about one hour late, at 16:15 hours. I must mention the ginger cat that took a fancy to us. A couple of saucers of milk and we had found a friend!

The temperature is around 30 degrees C but with 100% humidity. Out of the breeze it is VERY oppressive. There is a Co-op store that stocks most groceries, cleaning products etc. It's expensive; e. g. one roll of paper towel $3. Other shops include a Surf Shop at the Airport, Ferrel Shop and Dive Shop that opens for short periods only, at peculiar times.

First impressions of the atolls were of beautiful shades of aqua coloured water (even though it was cloudy), lovely sandy beaches, lush tropical palms and undergrowth on the island. The shelter for yachties on DI, that I had read about and seen in photographs, was there. We contacted Dieter and eventually he turned up at 1100 with Mohamed (the policeman) in an aluminium runabout. They both came aboard and the official questions and papers for clearance were dealt with. My maiden hair fern (plant) had a "HOLD QUARANTINE' sticker on it and necessitated a page of questions and a signature from the skipper. Seems my plant isn't really mine at all! Once we were cleared and the authorities had left we launched the dinghy to go ashore. The weather had calmed down and it had stopped raining. Hermit crabs were scuttling everywhere and eating coconuts that were lying on the sand. John husked a coconut and we all had a drink of the coconut milk; it was sweet and delicious. We ate some of the flesh as well, very good. The shelter is covered in plaques made by people visiting DI in their yachts from all over the world. They were all very original and some very amusing. The two water tanks had been overhauled and made rat proof in 1995 by the Cocos Island Land Council. It is really good to have a supply of fresh water so close for showering, washing hair and clothes. We have rigged up a clothes line and wash everyday to keep the load manageable. It's just like Gilligan's Island!

After our shore excursion we returned to Clare very tired but happy and so thrilled we had arrived safe and sound. Clare certainly did us proud. clean skipper and crew retired to bed. The final nine hours run before we arrived at DI was 55nm.

The people living on West Island receive fresh produce sporadically by cargo ship and just before we arrived there was a period of four weeks where no fresh produce had been shipped to the island. fter making the 'Powers That Be' aware of their plight, a special flight was sent in for a couple of Wednesdays. Now a weekly flight on Saturdays and two weekly Wednesday flights will ensure fresh supplies in the future for the locals and yachties.

Cocos Island is duty free. Alcohol is very cheap.

With the plane arriving late, Nigel was concerned about the time we would get back to DI. We had to go to the ferry at West Island to get to Home Island, collect our dinghy and then cross the lagoon to Clare. A bus leaves the airport after the charter flight to take people to catch the ferry to Home Island. Darkness sets in about 6.30pm here and very quickly.

We saw Julie briefly – it was really good to see her and she was very relieved to see us. She said it was probably *just as stressful for family and friends at home waiting for news of our safe arrival, as it was for us fighting the elements. I wonder if it was really fair putting our family through the ordeal? Julie gave me letters from granddaughter Chelsea (which was my first real letter from her), my daughter Suzanne and my sister Glenice and brother-in-law Neil, plus photographs. Also included were some of my favourite biscuits, with a request from Chelsea to save two and eat them on her birthday, the 24th May. I bought her a locally crafted sterling silver starfish pendant and sent it back to Perth (with other letters) with one of the passengers leaving on the plane. Julie brought us a present of a ceramic cat with a kitten (really cute) – Puss Cat and Kitty - and a Cocos Island wind chime.*

We arrived at the ferry with time running out and it probably would have been ok had the ferry left straight away but unbeknown to us the bus made another trip back to the airport to pick up a second load of passengers. By the time we arrived at Home Island and retrieved our dinghy from the mooring, the light was fading rapidly. We found that the red safety thingy wasn't on the motor (Nigel could have improvised, we learnt later) and it was too dangerous to set off across the lagoon to Clare, a distance of about one and half miles.

We were sort of stuck with nowhere to go, as there is no accommodation on Home Island. We left all our stuff on a bench at the ferry terminal and walked to a phone box to phone Dieter, the Quarantine guy, to see if he could get a message to John about the dinghy. We were lucky and were able to speak to John who said the red thingy was on the motor when he left it. We came to the conclusion that kids must have been playing in and around the dinghy as there was also a lot of water in it. (Maybe not – the kids seem well-behaved)

We then had to decide where the best place was to spend the night – on the benches at the terminal or find a building somewhere. The latter appeared to be the better choice. A sign gave directions to a Community Centre, which could be a good bet. It was open and had chairs with lift off cushions that we could put on the floor to sleep on. Inside it was incredibly hot so we sat out on the steps to read our mail when one of those 4-wheel drive motorbikes, that everyone here drives, went by with two people on it. We thought that there may be a slight chance that they were looking for us so Nigel took off in pursuit. He caught up with them at the Ferry Terminal and yes, they had received a phone call from Dieter to rescue us! We piled on to their machine with our big bag of washing, a box of fresh food Julie had brought us and they took us back to their house. Their names are Dale and Rob. Dale is one of the nursing sisters who works between Home Island and West Island at the Health Centres. Rob has a job working on West Island. They have a son, Matthew. They gave us a drink and some food to eat and it was arranged that Rob would take his aluminium boat and lead us in our dinghy across the lagoon back to Clare. Just before we left Dale and Rob's house it started to rain but not too heavily. We went to the dinghy with Rob on his 4-wheel machine towing his boat. We got it launched and our stuff on board – the washing and box of food in Rob's boat. We then set off - (dumb, dumb thing to do!).

It was quite difficult to keep up with Rob and the wind seemed to be increasing. A sea was building as we progressed and we were taking on a lot of water. Our torch was a bit suss and about half way there a severe squall came across the lagoon and hit us and the rain came down in buckets, filling our dinghy faster than I could bail! By this time we were both becoming quite anxious and very, very wet through. We signalled to Rob and he came back and we decided to turn back and run with the sea and squall. Eventually, after arriving back at Dale and Rob's house one hour later, it was suggested that we stay overnight in the house next door because Jane, the Dental Therapist, who lives there, was over in West Island for the weekend. It was sort of a half way house for visiting health workers anyway.

It was fantastic to have a warm shower, and get into a dry bed. (It rained all night!) We were so grateful for the concern and help that was extended to us. Early next morning, after tidying up, we left and walked to our dinghy and motored back to Clare.

While we were at the house we took all our washing out of the bag to check if it had got wet – luckily no and we eventually got it all back on board Clare dry. That was some sort of miracle.

When we arrived back on Clare we had to set about drying her out because when John left for West Island, some of the portholes were left partly open and the carpet that had been put out to dry was sodden. It was two days before Clare was 'ship shape' again - just in time for us to go back across the lagoon to pick up Julie and John from the ferry. We walked around Home Island a bit – went to the Health Centre and Dale's house and she gave us a loaf of freshly baked bread. We also went to the Co-op and bought a couple of things. Potatoes and long life milk x3; total cost $13. Cost of salads that eventually find their way onto the Co-op shelves are very expensive e. g. Lettuce $6 each, tomatoes $10 kg, celery $8 each.

On the way back to Clare we all got wet again! Dale, Bob and Matthew came over in their boat to Direction Island and had afternoon tea with us on the Sunday.

Monday May 25th.

John and Julie's bags got wet on the way over including their video camera. The fresh fruit and vegies and scotch fillet and cheeses that Julie brought with her were a real treat. The four of us explored Direction Island and tried to dry out our clothes – not so easy in the humidity.

Tuesday 26th, Wednesday 27th, Thursday 28th and Friday 29th May:

Days were spent relaxing, reading, eating and drinking. Julie and John really good company and easy to get along with. John has caught (and Julie too) fish each day and we are enjoying them with our evening meal.

It has rained almost relentlessly for the past 4 days – the boat is becoming very wet and smelling musty. As I write it is Saturday 30th May, 09.45 local time (Cocos is one and half hours behind Perth) and it is raining again. The top portholes have to be closed and it becomes very hot and stuffy. We are all having trouble getting clothes dry. Towels are beginning to smell. Nigel isn't coping with all the damp very well and went to bed yesterday afternoon!

We all became very excited yesterday morning to see another yacht motoring into the anchorage. It is a French boat – registered in Noumea – named 'Plum de Cherve' with three guys on board. Poor things have been confined to their boat for 24 hours because quarantine and police couldn't come to Direction Island to clear them in yesterday because of boat trouble and inclement weather. Hope that we get to socialise with them. They don't speak very much English. As I write this, the clearance boat has just arrived and it is still raining. (09.55).

Saturday 30 May

Today we hope to take the dinghy to Home Island to have a walk around and have a look at the Clunies-Ross mansion. The sky looks to be breaking up so it may fine up.

Despite the rain we have been swimming every day and walking on Direction Island. We still haven't done 'The Rip'. Weather not good enough! The coral is spectacular at low tide – the yellow coral looks like big splodges of custard. There are hermit crabs everywhere – quite the scavengers, breaking into coconuts lying on the ground and getting into the rubbish pit. John uses them for bait. Besides them, there are little 'ghost' crabs at the water line and when disturbed run like the clappers into the water. Wild bantam roosters and chooks are about the only birds that I have seen. The sandy bottom of the lagoon is covered with sea slugs that are horrible if you accidentally tread on one. The water is beautiful for swimming – crystal clear, warm (30 deg C).

We have snorkelled to a wrecked fibreglass yacht on the bottom not too far from Clare. The story has it that it burnt to the waterline and sank. Spooky to see. Small reef sharks swimming around the wreck are harmless. A couple of turtles swam by and we saw a dugong.

I must make note of a yacht nearby, owned and skippered by A. and was the only other boat in the anchorage when we arrived. Nigel had been warned about a 'mad' woman on D. I. who has been here for 18 months and that the authorities are having difficulty moving her on. She is a very manipulative lady who made her presence known almost as soon as we arrived, wanting favours, acting peculiarly. She interacts mainly with males and talks very fast, not making eye contact. She frightens me and I refuse to have any contact with her. Now that the French boat has arrived we hope that she will turn her attentions in their direction. We have heard many tales about her – some probably exaggerated or made up but you can gather that things with her are not quite right. This morning, I was awakened by her crying or wailing loudly. Can you imagine sailing 1400 nm to a deserted tropical island in the middle of the Indian Ocean to be anchored close to a woman with mental issues? We are not sure what is her original nationality – she has an accent but she says she is Australian.

Saturday continued ... We did go to Home Island and walked around a bit. Went and had a look at the Clunies-Ross mansion. It is in a poor state of disrepair with some of the original furniture left in many of the rooms. The exterior is made of white bricks and all the rooms are lined with Malaysian teak. The entrance hall is very grand. High ceilings, big rooms, two storey. It seems an awful shame that such a beautiful house and grounds should fall into a state of neglect. The day turned out hot and sunny and it looks like we may have a rain-free day.

The Clunies-Ross Grand House on Home Island

The French boat was eventually cleared and the skipper and crew made their way to Home Island where we met up with them. Jacque is the skipper and Mark and Steven his crew. They were going to catch the ferry to West Island hoping to catch the Co-op open to get some food and drinks. They had taken 20 days to come from Darwin – 4 days without wind. They are heading for Djbouti. Saw a white Ibis at Home Island.

Another sobering sight was the wreck of 'Spanish Eyes.' They tried to enter at night (a no-no). The yacht had run aground on Home Island whilst attempting to enter Port Refuge. Nigel said they should have hove-to like us and waited until morning. What a terrible loss of an impressive yacht. It looked an expensive boat.

Wreck of 'Spanish Eyes' on Home Island

Nigel and I had a lovely snorkel over some coral and clamshells and lovely brightly coloured fish of all shapes and sizes. We made our way over to the Rip at the end of DI and spent many hours drifting over the coral – absolutely mesmerised by the myriad of sea life. Reef sharks were resting on the bottom but took no notice of us! I'm still battling with the washing but was able to air out the doona today.

A month later: Sunday 30 June

Sadly I haven't written for a month and I have lost track of days and what we did on what days."

That was Aileen's final entry before she flew home.

*****

One day, out of the blue, an ex-pat couple came aboard for a coffee and look-see. They were the island nurse, Lanie, and her partner, Lee. "Do you want to sell Clare?" they asked. I was flabbergasted. Sell Clare? After all the time and money that had gone into making this dream cruise come true – she was our floating home that we'd owned for seven years, so no, we didn't want to sell her. Then things occurred that made me change my mind.

Firstly, Aileen was not sure she could continue on without John. After lots of agonising, she announced, "I just can't sail on. I love coastal cruising but I don't like these long ocean passages. I just can't do it. I'll meet you in the Maldives. "

It had been pretty horrible for her in the rough sections and I could sympathise. I didn't want to sail on by myself. Aileen and I had become a tight team handling the vessel together. She would steer *Clare* and I would do all the sail handling and deck work. *Clare* is a big, heavy boat and needs a strong crew. Offers to join me were made from sailing friends back at Hillarys Yacht Club but, whilst I was considering all this, a second sobering event took place.

Secondly, we couldn't start the engine. The starter motor packed up and, with an 80HP diesel, there are no de-compression levers so that it could be turned over by hand. With no engine to charge the battery banks, there would be no autopilot, and the other electrics would gradually wind down too. The solar and wind generation couldn't cover all the power needs – especially the anchor winch. Aileen had flown back to Perth and a guy on another yacht came over and helped me get the starter motor off. I took it over to the workshop on West Island but they couldn't fix it, as it was a 24-volt system. It had to go back to Perth.

I took the charter flight back to Perth and left the starter with an auto-electrician in Balcatta to check out. Lanie was on the same flight and again asked me if I'd sell. The seed was planted and, with Aileen not wanting to continue, the idea began to take root insidiously in my mind. I was feeling like a traitor to *Clare* but didn't really think that the offer was serious at that stage.

"We still want your boat!" Lanie said.

"Ok, let me discuss it with Aileen, "I replied.

The phone rang the next day. "I've got your cheque!" It was Lanie. I asked her to give us a bit more time to think about it. A week later,the phone rang again, "Do you want to sell *Clare*?"

"Ok," I replied, "she's all yours. "

My reasoning was that, as Aileen didn't really want to go on, it was a reasonable offer and I realised that we'd been spoilt by having a third crew in John to help with the deck work. I was not sure about asking anyone else, even though friends were keen to help. We had sailed successfully as a couple for seven years, so I was confident that we could do it but thought that Aileen wasn't. On hearing the decision to sell, Aileen was speechless as she'd almost made up her made to fly back to Cocos with me to continue the cruise.

I flew back up on my own and we re-fitted the re-conditioned starter motor. I turned on the key and 'clunk' – the engine still wouldn't turn over. Bloody hell! Lanie and Lee came over to DI in their runabout and I explained the situation to them, but they still wanted *Clare*.

Lee and the island mechanic, Jack, came over in their boat on the next weekend with a big bag of tools and proceeded to take the head off the engine.

We found saltwater in the cylinders and the pistons seized solidly. So that was really the straw that broke the camel's back – I could not fix the engine myself.

After much hard work and swearing, the boys got the pistons out and took them and the cylinder head over to West Island to be cleaned and re-machined.

Salt water in the engine – disaster!

How the hell did that happen, I kept asking myself? I was perplexed at how the salt water had got into the cylinders. DI is a very beautiful, calm anchorage. We'd had *Clare* for seven years and sailed her in some very rough weather and never had any trouble.

Then I began to suspect A: the strange lady living alone on her own yacht that Aileen describes in her log. She would come over to our boat every afternoon demanding beers. The police on West Island had banned her from buying alcohol as she became unmanageable when drunk. We would give her just one beer but she kept demanding more, becoming abusive and angry if we refused. I put two and two together and reckoned that she'd sneaked over on to *Clare* whilst we were away over at West Island and poured sea water into the engine air-intake. We couldn't prove anything. It's a mystery we'll never solve, but I'm pretty sure that's what happened. We later found out that A. had also been a pest when anchored at Christmas Island. The locals got so fed up with her that they took the hat round to collect the money for a bloke to sail with her to Cocos (the money was for his air-fare back to Christmas Island). His account of that trip was not flattering, and he couldn't wait to get off the boat once they'd anchored at DI.

Lee and Jack worked on the engine for many months and eventually put it all back together and got it going again. I helped out with some parts but they did all the labour themselves in their spare time, saving lots of money.

So that was it: we'd sold *Clare*. She looked a picture in the anchorage there at DI and I was very upset at leaving her as I drove the ducky over to Home Island for the last time. There she was, ready for more ocean adventures.

"Goodbye, old girl!" I called out to her with tears in my eyes, "Look after your new owners."

My last teary view of Clare at DI before I flew home

The charter flight flew low over the atolls and I could see *Clare* in the lagoon below and there were more tears as I caught my last glimpse of her.

Chapter Three

Clare's History

"Jobs fill your pocket but sailing adventures fill your soul,"
                                                Jamie Lyn Beatty

After the saga with the broker who had sold us *Clare*, I was curious to learn more about her history. She was, after all, a fine example of Western Australian wooden boat building. Some digging revealed that a bloke called Hughie Holm, of South Perth, had built her by 1951 (construction probably began about 1948).

1951 – Launching Day at South Perth

South Perth 1951 – she has the tall oregon masts

The old hand-written records at Royal Perth Yacht Club are still available, and a visit to the club enabled Aileen and I to locate the original yacht register, all very neatly entered in a beautiful hand. She was listed as *Judith Clare,* designer Maurice Griffiths, the well-known English yacht designer. Well, we now knew for certain that she was not an Arthur Bishop (WA) design and build.

I wrote to Maurice Griffiths to try to obtain some line drawings for *Clare.* After some time, back came a rather indignant reply to the effect that some 'Down Under' designer had pinched one of his designs and had modified it, thus paying no royalties. Back in the early '90s, Maurice was a sprightly 91-year-old but he could still remember every design he ever produced.

More phone calls to the City of South Perth failed to find any trace of Hughie Holm, the builder. We don't know why such a large ketch was built for Swan River sailing. *Clare's* first owner was the then Danish Consul, Mr Odgaard and we believe the boat was built especially for him. His wife, Mrs Odgaard, who was still alive in 1991, told us how they went out into the South West forests to choose the jarrah trees that *Clare* was to be built from. The ornate woodwork that decorated the cabin was also cut from WA timbers. Mrs Odgaard mentioned that personal monogrammed linen was featured on board too. Old photos revealed that she was built as a fairly flat-decked boat with a large open cockpit. The family owned her for about five years before selling her to Bill Riley. Unfortunately, he'd passed away at the time of my research – along with many of the original members of Royal Perth Yacht Club. He had registered her with the club in 1957. It's still a mystery finding out why Bill bought *Clare*. We did discover that she had towering Oregon (Douglas Fir) masts and was raced on the Swan River in the 50s and 60s. At that time, *Judith Clare*, *Vivian of Struan* and *Gelasma* were most likely among the largest local yachts on the Swan River.

She was entered in the Naturalist Race in 1957 but was forced to retire. I believe the problem was that her tall rig overpowered her. The Oregon masts were replaced by shorter aluminium spars but the timber booms were retained. The aluminium masts are still on the boat and were in good condition at the time of writing (2021). I wonder what happened to those lovely Oregon masts?

She passed into the next owner's hands in the mid-60s. He is another mystery man. He moved address so many times it was impossible to track him down. Maybe someone who reads this book may be able to shed some light on *Judith Clare's* early owners?

We found out that a James Davey was another owner. In his (1971) membership application to RPYC, he states that he is, "in the process of restoring *Judith Clare* and was hoping to race her in both river and ocean races."

He apparently lost interest in her, and she was sold to three young blokes who lived on board at Two Rocks. They must have had lots of fun and parties! This was in the 70s when Alan Bond was using Two Rocks Marina to trial his first America's Cup yachts. Two Rocks would have been a lively harbour in those heady days but it is pretty quiet these days. *Judith Clare* was painted a distinctive blue back then but was becoming neglected as a sailing vessel by the young guys.

Clare painted blue in the early 80s (Rottnest Island)

Along comes Murray France, the next owner. Murray was really helpful when it came to tracing *Clare's* origins. He restored her and soon had her sailing again. In 1979, he installed a new engine – an 80HP Ford Sabre Marine Diesel. This engine is still on the boat and has been rebuilt twice since then. It still runs well. Murray had *Clare* for about five years and cruised her regularly to

Rottnest and up and down the WA coast. His wife didn't like the *Judith* part of the name, so the Frances were the ones to shorten it to *Clare*. Murray was the owner who installed the doghouse – an excellent addition and one that helped us in our decision to buy the boat.

Tragedy Strikes!

The next owners to enter the picture were 'The Doctors' – Drs Farmer and Watson. They purchased *Clare* for $37,500 in 1979. From around this time, she gained an aura of mystery. She became thought of as, 'a vessel with a chequered history.' The reputation was totally undeserved, but rumours do stick. The Doctors cruised and raced her out of Fremantle Sailing Club.

By 1984, Dr Watson had accepted a post in Queensland and plans were made to sail *Clare* to Brisbane via Darwin – sailing 'over the top' in the winter – the dry season. He bought new sails, installed Satellite Navigation and HF (high frequency) radio. She was repainted white, and with her large areas of varnish work and teak decking, she looked beautiful.

With a crew of two, Dr Watson set off from Fremantle in July '84 but ran into a severe nor-westerly storm a day or two later. The skipper decided to run with the storm and *Clare* was driven 90 nm south of Fremantle, close to Bunbury. After the wind abated and shifted to the south-west (as fronts tend to do on the West Coast), they re-set sail and headed north again. However, the young person on watch (Dr Watson was down below sleeping) somehow misinterpreted the Rottnest Lighthouse light and the transit lights for South Passage, and she struck a reef near Green Island at Rottnest Island. The crew had been trying to locate the lights for South Passage (the safe southern passage is a way into Fremantle for smaller vessels).

Disaster! Clare on the reef at Green Island, Rottnest Island, 1984

The skipper and crew took to the inflatable and scrambled across the reef to safety but poor *Clare*, listing badly, was stuck. Daylight revealed the ketch almost high and dry. The media were soon there in force to record the dramatic event. A local fisherman at Mindarie Marina, who was first on the scene, told me that, at this stage, *Clare* only had a small hole abaft the engine, on the starboard side but she was badly holed when the salvage gang tried to drag her off the reef.

"It was a botched-up job," he explained. "I advised them what to do but no one would listen – that's why she was holed. They even managed to damage the other side as they dragged her over the reef the wrong way without any sandbags."

She was dragged along the bottom of the bay to the little jetty at Green Island. There were several dramatic photos of the incident on display at the Rottnest Police Station (I have included some in this book). Divers managed to patch her up and she was re-floated and towed back to Fremantle Sailing Club. She was lifted out and deposited on the hardstand and declared repairable.

Clare was dragged over the wrong way – increasing the damage

The salvors, having bought her, 'as is, where is' for the paltry sum of $1.00 (one dollar), sold her to a bloke called Ron Wilson for an undisclosed sum. Ron had *Clare* repaired properly by a qualified shipwright but the old girl had earned a stigma since the drama. (We didn't know anything about all this when we purchased her in 1991). People were saying, "… but isn't that the yacht that sank at Rotto?"

She has been professionally marine surveyed four times (the last time by us) since the tragedy and was given a clean bill of health each time. She's very sound.

I received a letter from Dr Watson describing the incident and could tell that he was highly embarrassed by the whole sorry saga. To add insult to injury, the insurance company had to be taken to court before they paid out – but then sea-lawyering does have an odious reputation. (Witness the Suez Canal drama after that container ship *Ever Given* blocked the canal for a week after getting stuck across it recently).

Clare was on hardstanding for nine months while the repairs were carried out. During this time, another very strange incident occurred. One day, the normally pretty quiet work area was disturbed by the sound of a diesel engine running. The noise was coming from *Clare!* Close inspection revealed that the engine had started itself – maybe she was keen to get back in the water? Somehow, the starter motor had shorted out and had turned the engine over. Luckily no damage was done as the motor was shut down quickly.

The next owner after Ron Wilson spent a small-fortune refurbishing the interior, altering the steering position and installing expensive electronics. The only problem was that he and his wife found her to be quite a handful to sail so *Clare* spent most of her time in her pen at the Fremantle Sailing Club. That sort of thing added to her reputation. The final owner before ourselves again spent big bucks on further restorations. He did get to sail her quite often and loved her, but the 'recession we had to have' hit his business hard and he was forced to sell her. And that, of course, is where our adventures as owners began.

*****

The improvements we made to *Clare* improved her sailing characteristics immensely. I had full-length battens added to the mainsail. I divided the foresail into two. We installed a staysail with a furler on the inner stay, and I had the big genoa cut down into a yankee to set from the end of the bowsprit. She looked lovely under this rig and was much easier to handle, being well balanced now.

If you can imagine your car or bike with its gears – well, having a choice of sail to raise, it was a bit the same. If the wind piped up, we could reef the main, if it kept piping up, we could douse the main completely and continue under mizzen and headsails.

In really strong winds, I'd take down the yankee and we'd sail comfortably under mizzen and staysail. That's what made her such fun to sail.

Another job was to slightly increase the area of the rudder to give it more 'grip' on the seas. This improved the hydraulic steering no end, making it far less tiring to be constantly correcting to keep on course. We added an expensive autopilot to drive the rudder and that was a real luxury – *Clare* could now steer herself for hours on end with no one on the wheel.

***We extended the rudder
to improve her steering***

The finished job – it made a huge difference to Clare's handling

So yes, we can add ourselves to the list of other owners who spent lots of money on her. She was like a jealous mistress who needed showering with gifts all the time!

During the seven years of our ownership, we had so much fun. We sailed her up and down the coast, over to Rottnest many times and down south to Quindalup a few times. We found *Clare* to be a lovely vessel to live on. The portholes around her hull provided natural ventilation and cooling and it was a delight to sit at the saloon table watching the sea outside. While we built a new home at Hillarys, we actually moved onto the boat and lived on board for twelve months at Hillarys Yacht Club. That was fun - even in the winter gales – that is, except for that awful storm of 1994 that blasted in at over 70 knots. It was hell on board. The gunwale was driven under the jetty and burly club members had to help us extricate ourselves. Aileen couldn't get down the jetty in the huge winds and had to have assistance. We lost two friends, Paul and Sarah, in that storm. Their ferro-cement ketch was driven onto reef near Cervantes and broke up. Their bodies were never found.

Something Aileen and I are both very proud of was setting up *Cruising in Company* at Hillarys Yacht Club. Lots of yachties who were not into racing were just cruising about on their own. We formed a group of like-minded sailors and we cruised together to all ports north and south. We arranged radio skeds between the yachts, appointed a 'cruise leader' for events who had to plan the waypoints and work out any navigational hazards. Then we'd complete the day with a sundowner on a chosen vessel. *Clare* was often the one chosen as she was the biggest in the fleet in the early days and had wide side decks and a large cabin top for sitting on. Meetings were held every month in the HYC clubhouse. There would be a briefing on the proposed cruise, a guest speaker on a sailing/boating topic and a meal beforehand. The idea really took hold and we had large numbers attending. Aileen and I were made 'Cruise Captains' for the first three years from 1993 – 1997. The *Cruising in Company* group still flourishes at the club today.

One fun cruise I recall in *Clare* was the annual coastal cruise to Quindalup that was organised by Fremantle Sailing Club and South of Perth Yacht Club. The cruise from Hillarys Yacht Club was split into four legs: Hillarys to Fremantle, Fremantle to Mandurah, Mandurah to Bunbury and finally Bunbury to Quindalup.

Sailing south to Quindalup

Aileen enjoying perfect sailing conditions - 10-15knots of breeze

Well, on the Mandurah to Bunbury leg, we had a pretty strong easterly so the fleet got going about 04:00. Once vessels round Cape Bouvard, the coast is fairly straight, so yachts can hug the beach and sail in calmer seas. I put up all the rag (full sails) and *Clare* charged off, leaving many of the 'plastic' (fibreglass) yachts in her wake. Aileen and I sat on the cabin top waving as we roared along! That evening, skippers had to come up with a poem about the voyage for a fun competition – here is mine:

Quindalup 1993

We set off from Hillarys with much shaking of knees
It was 05:30 and there was a hell of a breeze!
Clare was eager to get to sea
So were her crew and skipper, that's me!
We hoisted the stays'l, the wind was so strong
Aileen exclaimed, "It very much hurts!"
As Clare raced south with a lift of her skirts.
We fetched Mandurah late afternoon
The first leg was over, all to soon
No sooner had we dropped our pick
When Aileen, cried, "We've got a visitor – quick!"
He turned out to be Rory Riley, by gum
Of Clare's second owner, he was the son.
He climbed aboard with a laugh and a smile
And told as a lad he'd sailed many a mile
On Judith Clare as she was then known
"She's a vessel you should be proud to own,"

He said over a beer - in his eye was a tear,
As he recounted her past.
Next day, we said, "Goodbye" at last
Weighed anchor – it weighs a ton!
Enough to break your back in the midday sun
With mains'l and mizzen drawing just right
And with our two headsails, she is a beautiful sight.
We passed Cape Bouvard off to port
By now we were really enjoying our sport!
Clare on a reach is hard to catch
'Plastic fantastics' were left in our wake –
"Catch Clare, catch Clare for goodness sake!"
I heard skippers cry out on 27. 94
We then passed an SS34 – boy was she sore!
Bunbury Harbour was fetched by two
Sails furled, it was time for the crew
To step ashore and sample the local brew.
Who should we greet, I kid you not –
It was that man Trevor - Mr Yacht Grot!
Our vessel, and probably yours too
Is full of bartered bits, some even new.
So we laughed when we saw the biggest yacht in the fleet
Yacht Grot is by far, the busiest shop in that street!
We stayed a day extra in Bunbury, the hospitality was great
But a day longer, we could not wait.
For Quindalup was beckoning with white beaches and sand

So we weighed anchor at five and soon lost sight of land
We set our last lure on 50 metres of line.
The weather was perfect, all was just fine
Next minute, off my perch I nearly fell -
From Aileen came a tremendous yell!
"I've got one, I've got one – it feels big to me.
It's two feet long with jaws like a vice
This one's for breakfast, I bet he'll taste nice!"
Into the pan, as quick as you like,
Went this delicious, tasty fresh pike.
The haze was up – where is our port?
To the chart and GPS we had to resort,
But at last, there it was dead ahead
A chance to get some sleep after going to bed.
But as soon as we got in
What is that bloody great din?
It's 27. 94, cackling away
With gossip and natter all bloody day!
So to the sailors who spend all day on the air
It's enough to make a skipper pull out his hair!
Now our next port will not be Quindalup, Carbunup,
Metricup, Manjimup or Meelup –
it will be the quiet anchorage at
"SHUT UP!!"
Just kidding folks – thanks for inviting us along
'Cos we do like being part of this madding throng!

That piece of 'poetry' provoked lots of jeering and catcalls from the plastic yacht skippers but we did win the bottle of red as a prize!

(Note: 27. 94 is a 27meg marine radio channel for boat to boat communication).

****

The family loved our boat. *Clare* had plenty of room, wide side decks and flat cabin tops making parties on board easy to organise. We loved taking our grandees sailing – Chelsea was not a boat lover and would cry, "Nigel we're going to sink!" Or, "Nigel, we're going to tip over!" The best way to calm her down was to put her on the helm – which she really enjoyed – and that stopped her complaints. Once at anchor, she was quite happy on the boat but never really enjoyed the sailing.

Chelsea

On the other hand, Adam, our grandson, took to sea life like a duck to water. He loved fishing and always had a line out to catch us some lunch or dinner. When he came on board with his smelly bait, I used to sit him in the dinghy on a long painter off the back of the boat to keep the stench at bay! He was quite happy sitting out there catching his fish. He has gone on to became a very proficient angler and free-diver as an adult and is the part owner of a spear fishing business, called *Spear West*. We like to think his early experiences on *Clare* had a great influence on him.

Adam

I guess it was after about four years with Clare that we began to think about a longer ocean sail, as mentioned earlier. Lots of our friends and club members helped with the preparation. There were so many details to attend to and there was always that niggling feeling at the back of your mind that you'd forget something.

*After stripping all the old paint off,
the jarrah was pristine underneath after 44 years!*

One huge job we tackled was burning off all the old hull paint, above and below the waterline. I and a fellow wooden yacht owner, Bill, did this over three days of non-stop working – burning and scraping off all the old paint. When we'd finished, we stood back and were amazed at the lovely quality of the jarrah under all that paint: it was still pristine after 44 years. That beautiful pink jarrah was just as immaculate as it was when she was built in 1951 – testament to that fantastic West Australian timber. I recalled that Mrs Odgaard had told me that they actually went into the South West jarrah forests to pick out the trees for *Clare*. There is no way that you could do that today – the trees are not there in numbers now, mainly due to the disease called 'die back' and extensive logging – and also the expense would be prohibitive.

On hard standing – the lovely lines of a very stable hull

After repainting her white with black antifouling she looked a treat and many people stopped by for a chat and to admire her lines. We were proud owners. It's a funny thing – even the most die-hard landlubber loves wooden boats and wants to know about them.

Another major undertaking was to re-condition the engine. Bob, the owner of *Toroa* (she was to become our second timber yacht one day in the future) was a prison officer and he was able to get his inmates to overhaul the motor. The prisoners did a great job. All we had to do was supply them with cake (with files in them of course!), some tobacco and give them lots of praise. Most of them were guys trying to get back into society. Many had low self-esteem and really appreciated my visits to Casuarina Prison to chat to them about progress with the engine. The engine was delivered back to *Clare* painted a lovely blue and had been completely re-conditioned. It was a fairly inexpensive way to tackle the job, as the labour was obviously free!

We had seven wonderful years having fun with *Clare*. Every

summer holiday we would sail over to Rottnest to anchor in Longreach Bay with many other yachts. There were five fairly large yachts in the anchorage and we'd always anchor close to each other in the 'back row,' as we called it. We all became good friends and would take turns to host the sundowners. It all became something of annual event. One night early in our ownership, a particularly strong easterly came up around midnight. I got up to check the anchor and found that we were dragging slowly down the bay to its western end!

"What are you guys doing?" enquired Jane on *Manyana* as we moved slowly past!

"Oh, just checking!" I laughed. We fired up the engine and re-anchored, letting out more chain and she was ok.

Another very interesting voyage was an overnighter down to Quindalup. These two young blokes needed some sea-time and distance sailing to earn their Offshore Skipper tickets from Yachting Australia. I said they could use *Clare* but informed them they were going to have to plan the whole exercise – including provisions/cooking, navigation, sail changes, watches and so on. I would just be the adjudicator and not suggest anything (but would have to take control if a dangerous situation came up). The guys were great. They did the lot – fed and watered me all the way while I took notes. On arrival at Quindalup, we had some breakfast, then upped anchor and sailed straight back to Hillarys. The boys passed with flying colours and I was a very pampered skipper (or admiral) on that trip.

One of *Clare's* attractions was her motion in a seaway. Being heavy with rounded bilges, she never bashed her way through seas, just shouldered them out of her path – unlike many modern designs with flat bottoms. Those sorts of fibreglass hulls tend to bang and thump their bows in a seaway. *Clare* is what old salts would call a 'good sea boat.' She was comfortable.

That damn plank!

Every wooden vessel seems to have a leak. Well, in *Clare* it was in her for'ard sections and we could never quite trace it to caulk it up. We installed a little electric bilge-pump to suck the water out. That was ok but I was determined to find that leak, so on one annual haul-out, I contacted a shipwright who'd been working on the *Endeavour* replica, to have a look. He was an old boy from England named Fred. He scratched his head and said, "We have to replace a plank."

After lots of wrestling, we cut the old plank out and fitted a brand new piece of jarrah. Fred planed and sanded the piece until it fitted perfectly and finished the job with some professional caulking.

"Let 'er take up for a few days, and she'll be fine," he said. (Wood expands in seawater and that makes the planks watertight). After a month, we still had that little leak.

"Ah!" Fred exclaimed, "she shouldn't have done that!"

So we learnt to live with the leak.

For electrical power generation, we installed a couple of solar panels to the doghouse rooftop and a wind generator to the mizzen mast. Between them, they produced quite a lot of power and we didn't have to run the engine at anchor, which was quite a relief. The wind genny was a bit noisy in strong winds so we'd shut it off at night. That stopped other boats nearby from complaining and gave us a better sleep too. I found it fun to watch the ammeter needle creep up with the wind as amps were pumped into our large battery banks. We were quite energy sufficient for most needs and 'green' back then in '98.

Clare in the News

Clare seemed to enjoy being in the papers! Firstly, there was that horror story of the doctors. Then Aileen and I were featured at the annual Wooden Boat Show in Fremantle in 1993. We were photographed down below in *Clare's* comfy saloon. That show was a lot of fun as we had *The Storyville Jazzband* playing up on deck during the day, creating lots of excitement.

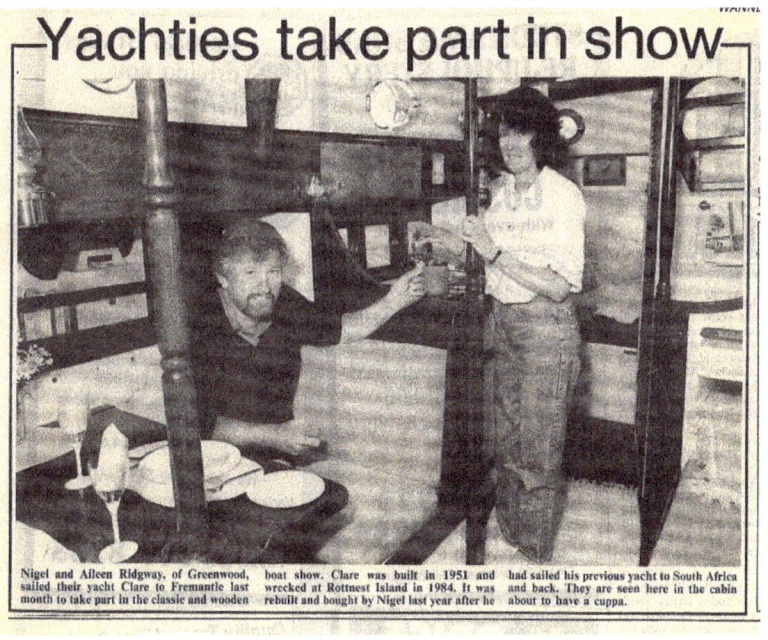

We enjoyed fending off lots of questions about Clare!

The third article was in the Sunday Times. This was a double-page spread that was about live-aboards at Hillarys Marina. A few couples were interviewed about the lifestyle and how we coped living small. We had a very wind blown photo taken for that story!

One more amusing incident (in hindsight – not at the time) was another cruise back from Quindalup. We invited my nephew and sister-in-law to sail with us – I assured them it would be a 'doddle' with a downwind run all the way home to Hillarys Yacht Club. Never tempt fate with the promise of fine weather for rellies. We set off at about 16:00 from Meelup, having picked up our extra 'crew' from the beach there. All was well in the lee of Cape Naturaliste, but as soon as we cleared the Cape, up pumped the wind and swells and it was 'hang on'. We surged along happily for some time but during the night, the fitting for the spinnaker pole on the mast broke and the pole went skywards! The yankee was thrashing about so I had to climb out onto the bowsprit to douse it, and get the pole down to lash it on the foredeck. By this time, the bowsprit was arching through about 15 feet of up and down motion with the swell. By the time I'd got everything sorted, I needed to feed the fish urgently! After a huge spew, I retired below exhausted, leaving Aileen and her sister to con the ship.

"Just keep the moon in that doghouse window," I said before I disappeared. The girls were great. Aileen had already sailed *Clare* (as skipper) to Rottnest with our daughter, Suzanne, and had sailed with a girlfriend, Angela, from Fremantle to HYC – so she knew what she was doing without me. The wind eased by morning and we had a nice quieter run up the west side of Garden Island, through South Passage and on to Hillarys. I don't think Glenice (Aileen's sister) has ever forgiven me for that night. We never again promised family fine weather if they came out with us.

Humpback whales are a feature of the waters between Rottnest and the metropolitan coast. Around October and November, they hang around in Gage Roads, resting their new calves before carrying on to Antarctica. In June and July, they head north and new calves are born up in the Kimberley, especially in Deception Bay. We had family on board for a day sail in spring when one huge humpback surfaced right alongside *Clare*. She turned on her side and swam with us for about half an hour, one huge eye staring at us. We all looked down into it and were mesmerised – there seemed to be so such wisdom and goodwill in that stare. Then she leisurely turned over and submerged.

Dolphins are another regular sight in our local waters and they would often come charging over to swim in our bow wave. I loved sitting out on the end of the bowsprit to watch them, laughing happily.

My favourite spot –
out on the bowsprit watching dolphins play in the bow-wave

Yes, *Clare* was a happy ship and gave us many wonderful memories. One of them was sailing over to Rottnest from Fremantle in a really strong easterly. I did this with Bob, the trombone player in the *Storyville Jazzband*, (I was the drummer). We put lots of sail up and *Clare* fetched Thomson Bay in an hour – that's 10 nautical miles in one hour = 10 knots of speed.

Fantastic! I got into trouble with Aileen when she arrived later in the day on the ferry, as we'd taken a bit of water and the saloon carpet got wet. I was never allowed to push her that hard again.

I can safely say that of the ten boats we had owned over 30 years, *Clare* was my favourite and it was a very sad moment when we had to let her go.

After some mourning, we bought a fibreglass S&S 34 that we owned for a couple of years. A lovely yacht to sail but a bit cramped down below, so we sold her to buy *Toroa*, a New Zealand-built 39 footer of timber/dynel sheathed construction. We sailed her 'Over the Top' to Queensland and NSW over two years. But that's another story. Lovely as *Toroa* was, *Clare* still continues to be my favourite.

Clare and Toroa –
two lovely wooden boats we had the pleasure of owning

Chapter Four

Lanie's Story

"There is nothing more enticing, disenchanting and enslaving than life on the sea,"

Joseph Conrad

Lanie, the Cocos Island nurse who bought *Clare* from us at Cocos, had her own amazing adventures in the old ketch. She takes up the story:

"Jeez, we must be sinking – the water is over the floorboards!"

Here we were off Langkawi, Malaysia, in a 50-year-old wooden boat that looked like she was about to sink on us! We pumped out the bilges like people possessed; we checked the seacocks, praying that the loo ones weren't left open. Phew! They were closed. Crew off the hook!

Many questions: where and how is the (expletive) water getting in? Is there a hole in the hull? Did we hit something without realizing it? Will everything down below be wrecked? Are we going to sink? Should we put out a MAYDAY?

Eventually, we found the source of the problem: seawater was coming in through the shattered stern gland (*Nigel's notes*: the stern gland is where the propeller shaft exits the hull and needs to be pumped with grease regularly to keep the water out and to prevent overheating if the prop is free-wheeling under sail). A temporary repair job was done, and we managed to hobble into Langkawi. That was the final incident in a chapter of near disasters in *Clare*, my 40-foot wooden ketch. Virtually a complete novice, I was now the owner of a classic timber yacht.

My story really began at Direction Island (DI), Cocos (Keeling) where I'd bought *Clare* from Nigel and Aileen in July 1998. I had been living there for three years as the community nurse. With a broken-down engine, they had no choice but to sell. My partner, Lee, and I set about repairing the seized engine, an exercise that seemed to take forever. Getting the parts and actually doing the work in a remote place like Cocos was an amazing feat in itself. With the goodwill of the local ex-pats and Coco-Malays, we were eventually able to re-condition the engine and re-install it on the boat. Many comings and goings between Home Island and West Island in our runabout in all weathers paid off and we got the engine going again.

Clare was on anchor at DI right through the cyclone season that year. One actually passed close to the atolls but, luckily, headed back out into the Indian Ocean again before hitting. *Clare's* anchor chain was ramrod tight in that blow!

By May 1999, we were ready to leave the atolls and upped anchor on 16th May, heading for the Chagos Archipelago and Diago Garcia. This was to be the first leg of our sail. That's about 1,500 nm (or 2,817 kilometres). We alternated our watches and settled into the sailing life.

Not too far from Cocos, I got a taste of what seasickness is like – it's horrible! But I did get my sea legs and the nausea began to subside and then I was able to appreciate being on the Indian Ocean with nothing but the elements of nature to enjoy. The wind was with us and we were travelling at comfortable speeds. The wind and swells moved our bodies from side to side – occasionally giving us a jolt! I soon learnt to keep one hand always in touch with the boat. The voyage was really good in the beginning before things went pear-shaped. We caught tuna, enjoyed doing the 'boat chores' and learnt to respect the ocean and our new home, *Clare*. We were in really good spirits, enjoying sundowners with wine as we bowled along, watching the seas that were sometimes quite big.

> *Day 21 (log): We have fair winds and are sailing across the Great Chagos Bank. Clare is cruising at 6 knots. I'm on the helm trying to keep a northerly course. I'm reflecting on the problems we've had on this leg: low battery power, a stuffed alternator, a lost solar panel in a gybe, water leaking through the stern gland and the hydraulic autopilot playing up!*

Lee searches the horizon for the Chagos group

"Land- ho!" What a buzz! We get our first sight of land in three weeks. It was Nelson Island. Our navigation must have been good as we were dead on course. We got closer to the island but it was too deep to anchor. We made our way across the lagoon with the exhaust screaming. It was overheating! Yachties at anchor heard us entering the atoll and there was lots of chatter and guidance over the VHF radio as we made our way in to where there was a beach. I was on the bow looking out for bombies. It was deep and very clear but you could see them sticking up on the seabed. It was great to have a welcome party to greet us and it was a huge relief to finally let go the anchor. We had a nice stay here – we went fishing with the other yachties and got to know them well.

**Lanie leaves a visiting card on one of Chagos' Islands.
(Very happy to be safely anchored after the dramas)**

Chagos Archipelago is owned by the British but is now an uninhabited group of 60 islands, except for Diago Garcia. It is a well-known and favourite anchorage for yachts crossing the Indian Ocean. The Americans have an important strategic air force base at Diago Garcia. At present, there is a lot of diplomatic goings on as the Mauritian government is laying claim to the Chagos group – and the British conservative government doesn't want to let them go.

After talking to fellow yachties, it seemed our best option was to sail to Gan in the Maldives, a place where we could get the alternator repaired. Originally, our destination was to be Rodrigues (near Mauritius), then onto Tanzania (Africa).

We made our way to Gan (Addu Atoll): it is situated 4 degrees from the equator and is the southernmost island in the Maldives group. It was an important Royal Air Force base until 1976, and is now part of the Maldives and relies mainly on tourism.

The ocean was like a millpond. We couldn't run the engine because of the fumes and a high-pitched screaming noise. Lee had an idea. He fitted the exhaust directly to the motor and it worked. We motored all night. Sixteen nm (nautical miles) from port, smoke and oil were coming out of the exhaust. The exhaust pipe had overheated. We managed to sail the last few miles to Gan. We sailed inside the lagoon to the causeway, then motored into the basin and dropped the anchor, breathing a sigh of relief – we had arrived! We were in a spot not far from a factory where clothes are made.

We ordered a new alternator from Perth, hoping it would arrive in two weeks. Not to be – it took four weeks. The rubber dinghy was looking the worst for wear too. Despite trying different types of glue, the bottom kept falling out! During our stay, we got to know the locals. Kids would come on board and we'd go fishing on the local longline boats. I'd never seen so many fish caught so fast, it was an amazing sight. I did a bit of touch-up painting on *Clare* while we were waiting for the alternator. Lee caught some crayfish (lobster). The local people were really nice there.

Our original plan to sail to Africa was no longer an option. We were very disappointed. So now we decided to sail to Sumatra, then onto Thailand where we were told we could get repairs done. After five weeks at Gan, we were desperate to leave – no money, no work and it was too hot. Finally the alternator arrived. We fitted it and made preparations to do clearance the next day.

Customs clearance took us three hours. We were excited to have a new alternator. Our power problems were over and we motored out of Gan happily but felt sad at leaving our new friends. We cruised in company with the yacht *Gitana* and that was fun. The 'Admiral' on *Gitana* was an excellent cook so our meals improved when we visited them.

The events that happened next tested us to our limits. We cruised along with the autopilot running and all systems working and were finally feeling confident. We hoped to fetch our destination in Indonesia within a week. Well, we were soon to discover that it doesn't pay to be too confident. Just nine hours out of Gan the engine stopped.

'Oh no''' I thought, 'what the hell could be happening?'

We discovered that the fuel tank had only 20 litres of the 150 litres of diesel left.

"Shit!" Total fuel on board was now down to 40 to 50 litres. Now we're not able to run the engine to charge the batteries. No batteries, no power, no fuel – what now?

We discussed our options: if we went back to Gan, we'd have to wait two more weeks (or more) for parts. If we continued to Sumatra (the island of Weh), it would take weeks to sail. We would have to hand-steer with no power but we would get to a place where we could repair *Clare*. After much deliberation, we decided to push on and head for Sumatra. The winds started light but as we made our way north, they increased. We lost radio contact with *Gitana*. We had a few days of rough sailing in winds of up to 40 knots. We continued with a reefed mainsail and the lee rail underwater.

Lee, a heavy smoker, ran out of smokes two weeks out. He craved chocolate. He wanted a Mars Bar out in the middle of the Indian Ocean – can you imagine that? So I made a chocolate cake in the pressure cooker. It hit the spot – we had coffee and chocolate cake – yum! So we soldiered on, the seas remaining rough, confused and rolly. The steering course was worsening. We were sailing too far south.

Then we were becalmed, 290 nm from Weh. It was our 18th day out from Gan. The main halyard broke – Lee climbed the main mast to fix it. The water was getting low, the food supplies were dwindling, the battery power low – and our MORAL WAS VERY LOW!

There was hardly any movement through the seas – we travelled only seven miles in seven hours. The sails were crashing around, driving us mad. Lee checked the batteries, and worked out we could save enough amps from one bank to start the engine. He said the other bank was so low, there was, "not enough power to pull the skin off a rice pudding!"

> *(Log) After 26 days, we were now going backwards with the ocean current. (The South Equatorial current). We were getting more and more desperate. We heard some chit chat on the radio. Lee tried to call them up but they refused to respond. I then had a go and as luck had it, we saw a ship heading south about four miles way. The captain responded to me but he was very wary and was worried that we might be pirates. Once he was satisfied that we really were in need of assistance, he turned the ship around and headed towards us. His crew dropped off a 44-gallon*

drum (220 litres) of diesel and two water containers off the stern. Lee put our ducky (without its bottom) into the water and went to retrieve the floating drums. I chatted to the captain and was completely oblivious to Lee, who now had to dodge a sea snake that was trying to get into the dinghy with him. He hurried back to Clare without the diesel – pale and trembling. I yelled, 'Where is the fucking diesel?" He was almost bitten but I sent him back. How the hell did we get that 44-gallon drum on board? Well, we roped it with our main halyard and winched it up over the side – it took all our strength. We were saved!

We now had 70 miles to go but we had an opposing current. We had drifted back 20 miles – even with the kite up full of wind. It seemed as if we were moving. We checked the GPS and *we were moving* – backwards! So we had to start the engine as we were back at the position we were two days ago. We slowly made our way to our destination, batteries charging and autopilot steering. Finally we sighted land - the island of Weh. Then the engine stopped. *What now?* This time is wasn't fuel – it was the fuel pump. We had a bit of wind, so we sailed and headed to the spot on the chart where the harbour was indicated.

I called up the harbour on Channel 16 but got no response. We sailed closer and closer – about 20 metres from the beach and in 6 meters of water. A self-appointed pilot boat came out and this guy yelled, "Go, Go, Go!" It seemed we were in the wrong place.

The wind started to push us closer to the rocks and shore but we had no idea that the harbour was just around the corner in what looked like a creek. Anyway, the pilot kept gibbering and yelling. "Go!" So we sailed into unknown waters at dusk – we had no choice. The pilot led us to a harbour that seemed nothing like what was on the chart. He wanted money – we didn't know how to handle it. He didn't want to leave our boat but eventually, after a smoke and coffee, he did. However, next morning, a letter was delivered to *Clare* again asking for money.

There we were in a foreign country with no water, fuel or money. But we loved it there in Weh and wished we could have stayed longer. The island is very pretty. The anchorage is not far from a seawall where you can get on and off the boat from your dinghy. It's hilly with an island in the middle of the bay. It had a bit of a third-world atmosphere – most locals living in shanties. We did a big tour and then I had to go to the mainland (Sumatra) to get some money from the bank. A ferry service plies between the island and mainland. Lee was ordered to stay on *Clare* as security to make sure we paid our dues. Customs and Immigration introduced us to a 'personal relations' guy who was going to make sure we didn't sail away without paying. However, there was nice cold beer there on the island and so we mostly enjoyed our time.

We calculated that it was only three more days motoring to fetch Langkawi. We took on an English backpacker, Suzie, who wanted a ride to Thailand. Having no charts of the area, we used Suzie's 'Lonely Planet' guidebook as a chart!

The next day was spent looking for the entrance to Ao Chalong, in Thailand. We managed it with the 'Lonely Planet' that had a little map of the town. Once in, Lee and I went into town and Suzie left the boat there with a little note saying, "I wish you guys luck and lots of fun for the rest of your trip. Signed: the slightly irresponsible, Suzie, the girl who boarded *Clare* for a quick 200-mile sail across to Thailand!"

We stayed there for about three weeks and then moved to the Yacht Haven Marina at Phuket to get shore power and some work done. It was a good move, giving us shore power, showers and easy access to get off and on the boat, luxuries we hadn't had for a while. We also enjoyed the other good things Phuket had to offer: great beaches, Phi Phi islands, banks, shopping, motels, cold cheap beer, movies, a HOT SHOWER and anything else we wanted. We even hired a car to explore some of the sights.

Most of our time was spent working on repairs to get *Clare* up to scratch so we could sail back to Melbourne. The hydraulic autopilot/self-steering was fixed. We hunted down a cheap second-hand inflatable dinghy – the Tinker Tramp 'life-raft' had been given a sea burial.

The electrics on *Clare* were too complicated to be fixed in Phuket.

Customs and Immigration have a 30-day limit on staying in Thailand. After we'd been there for our 30 days, we made our way to Langkawi in Malaysia, a three-day motor sail from Phuket Yacht Haven. On the way, we visited the lovely Phi Phi islands, relaxing and enjoying the beautiful waters, the unique fishermen and scenery. On the way to Langkawi, the incident described at the beginning of the story occurred. I was almost at the point of sinking the boat!

However, once we got in, it was not without another mishap. We arrived at the Langkawi Yacht Club but there were no berths available and we were desperate for shore power. We found out that the passenger ferry passed close to where we were tied up causing a huge surge that rocks all the boats. As *Clare* was moored on the very outer pontoon, before we knew it, she was lifted up and came down heavily on the pontoon. The gunnels were ripped to shreds! Now we were really pissed off but other yachties did come to assist us.

It became apparent that *Clare* and her crew were not really fit for the voyage back to Perth or Melbourne, so we sailed back to Thailand and put *Clare* up on the hard for major works in Surat Than Boatyard at Yacht Haven. This was when Lee and I both made plans to get some work. I left the boat and headed back to Perth in October 1999. Lee stayed on and waited for some of the repairs to be completed, then he secured a job as skipper on a

54ft catamaran sailing in Myanmar. We both felt *Clare* would be secure at Yacht Haven. We then made plans to return together to sail *Clare* back to Melbourne in about three or four months.

When Lee finished work in Myanmar, he returned to Phuket to find that the deck hadn't been sealed as we had requested. He tried to get the job done but to no avail, the deck still leaked badly when it rained. He then left Phuket Yacht Haven and sailed back down to Langkawi for port clearance. He had a very hard sail. Lee couldn't get the deck done, making it impossible to live on board the boat now. He secured *Clare* at The Moorings in Kitah, Langkawi with a bloke called Roger Prescott. So by December 2000, *Clare* was still moored in Langkawi.

Clare safely penned at Langkawi after more adventures.

Nigel: Here Lanie's story takes an even greater turn for the worse. Lee decided he'd had enough and went his own way as a charter skipper. Lanie was in a quandary about what to do next, so when she finally returned to Langkawi, she decided to get a fresh crew to help her sail back to Australia, making landfall in Darwin. However, that trip didn't work out well either and this part of her story ends in Singapore. She had further problems with the boat and crew and it was a huge relief to finally secure a berth in the famous Raffles Marina at Singapore. Here, she made the momentous decision to ship *Clare* home to Australia, securing her on a container ship at great expense.

Lanie had become desperate and was almost on the point of scuttling her boat – she became sick and very down but managed to get over it. *Clare* was eventually unloaded at Swanston Dock, Melbourne. That was in March 2001.

This has been a harrowing chapter of some awful events interspersed with a few pleasurable times. Many of their problems with the boat would have been due to the fact that she was anchored for 12 months at Direction Island (Cocos - Keeling). Sea air and saltwater are always a challenge for boats and to have *Clare* so long in that tropical humidity would not have helped the equipment on board. Fortunately, the next stage of Lanie's ownership was much more successful and pleasant.

Chapter Five

Lanie's Story from Melbourne to the Whitsundays

"Every island to a child is a treasure island,"
                                                        Richard Dawkins

Once unshipped and back in the water, *Clare* was motored to the Sandringham Yacht Club and put in the yard on hard standing. Lanie had made up her mind to keep the boat and restore her. This was another very significant decision and she spent "bucket-loads of money" (to use her expression) and much "blood, sweat and tears", but the finished job was remarkable, as you can see from the pictures.

Lanie looking very proud as Clare's owner/skipper

The refurbished doghouse looks amazing!

New paint-job at Sandringham Yacht Club

Clare was a going concern again by 2003. It had taken from 2001 to complete all the work. Lanie began to plan her next voyage. She was introduced to another lady, Pamela, an experienced racing sailor, and they made plans to sail to Sydney and then on up the New South Wales and Queensland coasts to fetch the Whitsundays.

All this activity caught the eye of a reporter and *Clare* was back in the news. This time, it was a good news story about the planned trip. *Clare* was given a blessing by a minister, with lots of family, friends and well-wishers in attendance. It was a great occasion. Lanie felt very proud of herself and *Clare*.

NEWS

An east-coast adventure into calmer waters

TWO women, a boat and Australia's east coast — it might sound like a formula for a new movie, but for Sandringham's Lenie Lester it has been a dream, four years in the making.

Last week Ms Lester, her first mate Pamela Harrison and her 12.5m wooden ketch *Clare* set sail on a personal journey of self-discovery and adventure.

The women will spend the next six months sailing up Australia's east coast, from Melbourne to the Whitsundays.

Ms Lester, 45, who bought *Clare* when she was working as a senior community nurse in the Cocos Islands, said she had dedicated the past four years to restoring it.

"I had never sailed before, but my partner was a sailor and he said he would help me sail the boat," she said.

"The plan was to sail to Africa, but our relationship ended and we only made it as far as Malaysia.

"Since then my dream has been to restore *Clare* and get her back on the water."

Ms Lester said *Clare* had become a big part of her life, even describing the boat as a friend.

"The goal of this trip is to put a lot of stuff behind me and turn all of this hard work into relaxation time," she said.

Her first mate Pamela Harrison, who has been racing boats for 12 years, said sailing a heavy wooden boat was going to be a challenge, but it was one she was prepared to meet.

"It was certainly a goal of mine for this year to look at ocean sailing rather than race sailing," she said.

"Lenie and I are looking forward to good weather and a lot of laughs."

Lenie Lester, left, and Pamela Harrison at Sandringham Yacht club.
Picture: SUSAN WINDMILLER

Clare is in the newspapers again

The girls added a professional skipper to the crew for the leg to Sydney. It was a successful trip. There were a few minor issues with the boat but overall it was fun and they met lots of interesting people.

Lanie and Pam preparing to leave Hastings, Victoria.
Note the beautiful hull after all the hard work Lanie put in

Setting off from Hastings, they made for Queenscliff, Victoria, and decided to take a break there before making for the Heads. She had heard shocking stories of yachts coming to grief sailing through that narrow passage to exit Port Philip Bay waters. As luck had it, they crossed the next morning with great tides, flat seas and excellent visibility. Lanie and Pam cracked open the first bottle of champers to mark the occasion!

They had a lovely sail to Wilson's Promontory and decided to rest a while before doing the big leg across Bass Strait. This was at the time when bushfires were raging at night and they could see the red blaze close to the coast as they headed for Eden. It was a moonless night. They made it safely in and waited a couple of days to get a window of good weather before heading for Sydney. It was a tremendous feeling of accomplishment sailing round South Head to make entry into beautiful Sydney harbour.

Clare heads for Sydney

A momentous occasion – sailing under Sydney Harbour Bridge

Again, the champagne was cracked open and the crew celebrated long and hard. They pinched themselves to be sure they were truly there. The girls toasted themselves on deck as they passed under that famous bridge. It was well deserved after all the traumas and problems earlier in Lanie's ownership. It was now 2005.

The hired skipper, John, left the boat after securing *Clare* onto a mooring at Blackwattle Bay, Sydney. From there, Lanie and Pamela made their way to Birken Head Point where another girl, Annie, joined the ship. After further preparations before heading off, they spent the night moored in gorgeous Rose Bay. It was now going to be their first sail without their 'notorious' male skipper. Lanie was officially declared skipper and the girls sailed on up to the Whitsundays on their own. This was a great achievement for Lanie as she gained more and more confidence in herself as skipper – and learnt to trust that *Clare* would look after them.

Upping anchor and once through Sydney Harbour Heads, they meandered through the Hawkesbury River and spent a few days exploring the most magnificent anchorages like Little Patonga, Cowan Point, Cottage Point and Smith's Creek – 'God's Own Country,' plus one of the loveliest anchorages on the whole east coast, Refuge Bay. It quickly became apparent to Annie that Lanie was spending lots of time checking the engine. Lanie quipped, "It's pretty uncomfortable in my g-string getting up close and personal with the motor!" This caused lots of merriment for the all-girl crew. The girls were having a great time. Annie eventually had to leave before the next leg to Port Stephens.

They fetched Port Stephens after an all-night sail but on entry, the engine failed. Lanie tried desperately to work her magic in the bilge again but this time, the motor refused to respond. They had to sail back out but luckily the seas were flat at the time. They called the Water Police to get a tow in. The police towed them to the public jetty where they had the best views in town. Water had seeped into the fuel tanks somehow, causing the shutdown. Whilst there, they also had the engine injectors serviced. A couple of days were spent exploring beautiful Port Stephens. The girls met the owners of a scenic cruise boat, Wally and Penny, who gave them a free ride along the Myall River where they enjoyed eating oysters and seeing the variety of birdlife. "It was very scenic," she said.

New South Wales rivers can be very difficult to enter as most have bars, and skippers have to work the tides to get upriver: the general idea is to wait until about three hours after low water, watch the seas then enter. Then the seas subside and there's much less chance of them breaking on the bars.

The pair sailed on up the coast to Coffs Harbour where, once in the marina, they were welcomed by other yachties they had met. Here they also met Kevin and his wife on their boat, an ex-prawn trawler named *Busy Girl*.

Lanie said that "Kevin and I got to know each other pretty well as we spent a few days together in *Clare's* bilge!" She was becoming known around the marina as, 'Bilge Lanie!'

Coffs is an excellent marina with first-class facilities. It was here that we arranged to have our other timber yacht *'Toroa'* trucked back to WA.

The girls had sailed for 32 hours straight before fetching Coffs, covering a distance of 150nm. By this time they had sailed a total of 1,000 nm since leaving Victoria. They named themselves the *'Clare Chicks'* and were becoming quite popular and well known amongst the yachting fraternity by now.

Other ports of call were Ballina and the Richmond River. They had no trouble crossing the bar (many boats – power and sail – have come unstuck on entry to Ballina, sometimes with loss of life).

The girls finally crossed into Queensland waters and had another excuse to crack open the champers.

Lanie and Pam celebrate crossing the tropic of Capricorn into Queensland waters –more champagne!

They made landfall at Southport where a pod of dolphins, on the bow, showed them the way in – always a good omen. Good anchorage was obtained at what yachties call, 'Bum's Bay' and they began to meet up with other cruisers and have fun. They were really enjoying themselves now. Queensland is a wonderful coast to cruise. We spent 18 months cruising there in *Toroa*, the other wooden yacht we had owned.

Lanie and Pamela must have been quite a celebrated duo as they sailed the Queensland Coast. *Clare* looked wonderful and many friends were made. Ports of call included Mooloolaba, Wide Bay Bar, Bundaberg, and Gladstone. Wide Bay bar is another tricky stretch of water to get you into Tin Can Bay and many yachts have come a cropper there on that bar as well. Lanie and Pamela sailed over the bar with no dramas.

She said the general plan was to sail about 5-6 nm off the coast to maybe lessen the effect of the east coast current which flows south and is stronger inshore at times. (*Alan Lucas in his NSW Cruising Guide actually recommends sailing much closer to the coast*). Once into Queensland waters, the South-East trade winds help to push you north.

Some steering problems caused them to sail into Rosslyn Bay (Yeppoon) where they hauled *Clare* out to fix things. Lanie said they had so much help from the blokes as two girls sailing were quite a novelty. After this episode, they had a lovely 10 days at Great Keppel Island, relaxing and really enjoying the cruising lifestyle.

Magic sailing in the Whitsundays

Other delightful anchorages they enjoyed were Pearl Bay, Island Head Creek, Hexham Island, the Percy Islands, Digby Island and Scawfell Island. The girls cruised in company with other yachties who were also from Melbourne; together visiting Brampton Island, Lindeman and Thomas Islands before finally dropping their picks (anchors) near the Whitsunday Sailing Club. Lanie says they'll go down in Whitsunday Sailing Club history as the ladies who sailed a classic 40ft timber ketch from Melbourne to the Whitsundays. Sailing buddies and mentors from Victoria came to greet them at the Yacht Club and great celebrations were held all round. It was a fantastic achievement.

The 'Clare Chicks' celebrating. They have become sailing legends now!

The Whitsundays are a concentration of the greatest number of islands on the Queensland coast, some 73 altogether. The group is actually the Cumberland Islands but they are commonly known as 'The Whitsundays'. In fact, the Whitsunday group is the northernmost of the Cumberlands, comprising Whitsunday Island, Hook Island and their smaller close neighbours. All the islands, except Hayman, Dent and Hamilton, are national parks, although tourist resorts do exist in their midst – these being on

South Mole, Lindeman and Long Island. The main commercial harbour is Shute Harbour and the main shopping area, recreational boat harbour and marina are at Airlie Beach. It's all fairly expensive so cruising yachties tend to anchor out in the islands, or opposite the Whitsunday Sailing Club.

By this stage, Lanie and Pam were sailing in tandem with a 60ft catamaran and the two boats had lots of fun exploring all the anchorages, resorts and islands. Lanie says *Clare* was quite an eye-catcher wherever they went, standing out amongst all the 'plastic' yachts that are chartered and sailed among the islands, many having very novice skippers in control. When we were there, we loved hearing the charter yachts calling up Base with problems like dragging anchors, blocked toilets and flat batteries! RIBs (rigid inflatable boats) were always in demand to go out and assist the hapless skippers.

Lanie describes this time of her ownership as the best and she and Pamela got on well. A lot of socialising went on with other yachts and much champagne was enjoyed. Pamela eventually had to leave the boat in the Whitsundays and Lanie made the decision to sail back south on her own. By this time, she was an experienced skipper, navigator, handy person and sailor who had mastered anchoring and picking up moorings single-handed.

She met a few locals back at the Whitsunday Sailing Club after Pamela had departed for Melbourne and here she arranged for other boaties to look after *Clare* while she headed overseas for eight weeks. On her return, Lanie had more fun exploring the resorts, islands and anchorages. *Clare* was certainly different from the average charter yacht and was a real eye-catcher, as mentioned.

Lanie eventually sailed back to Mackay and it was here she began to think about selling *Clare*. Some moves were made to put her on the market but a change of mind had Lanie sailing off on her own down the coast again. She says it was a magic time as she was 'Master and Commander' of her own vessel on the high seas.

Lanie is 'Master and Commander of Clare now – sailing solo, quite a feat. (excuse the pun!)

By this time, it was about October 2005. Regrettably, she did take on a bloke called Clark as crew at some point but he turned out to be pretty useless, more of a passenger and nuisance than the sailor he pretended to be.

Unfortunately, the trip south turned sour when *Clare* developed another leak and she began taking on water near the Percy group of islands. Luckily, Middle Percy has a place where yachts can take the bottom and tie-up to a pontoon for careening at low tide. It's tricky to accomplish but Lanie managed it and made some temporary repairs to stem the leak – using some plywood, a caulking gun and Sikoflex. It looked as though some of the bow planking may have come loose. *Clare* was successfully floated off at high tide, ready to make her way south again. Clark did nothing to help during this episode – he just decided to walk around the island! Lanie was beginning to realise he was a user and a bit of a conman. She dubbed him 'Shrek!' – from the movie. She was again having thoughts about selling the boat, or even abandoning her at the Percys, but once afloat again these negative thoughts were put aside and Lanie prepared to move on.

Lanie retraced her steps south and revisited the lovely anchorages and ports she and Pamela had enjoyed on their way north. She described this time of her ownership of *Clare* as the most rewarding. She and Clark eventually fetched Newport Marina north of Brisbane where she bade farewell to him. He hadn't been much help on the voyage. It was Christmas Day and Lanie was greeted by other yachties who probably felt a bit sorry for her. Lanie says she was spoilt with kindness. After a bit of time at Newport, she shifted *Clare* to the nearby Scarborough Marina.

"It was there that I decided it was time to sell," she remarked to me over the phone. "You just get a feeling that the time was right to find the right person to do *Clare* justice. I'd done my best and restored her to where she was with what I could afford financially, physically and emotionally. A single nurse's salary is ok but not enough to truly make *Clare* a seaworthy vessel again – able to sail the oceans. I'd had a lot of fun and lots of dramas and felt it was time to move on. I'd heard that Scarborough was a good place to sell," she added in that call.

So *Clare* did go on the market. She took a bit of time to sell but eventually an offer was put in by a bloke called Martin. He owned a scaffolding business and was prepared to put money into *Clare*. He had worked with timber boats and had even restored one of his own when overseas. Lanie says he replaced some ribs (she had already replaced four or five) and stripped her back to the original timber. That was around December 2006. He kept her in Scarborough Marina for 12 months or more and had plans to sail from there back to Victoria. Apparently, he pulled out the engine and overhauled it and put in a new engine hatch.

From 2006 on, it has been difficult to trace what happened to *Clare*. I was not able to contact Martin to hear about his time with the boat. Rumour has it that his business went broke and he was bankrupted. Somehow, *Clare* ended up in Westernport Marina in Victoria again. Martin has a property on French Island at Hastings.

Lanie crewed for Rob, the owner of the yacht *Chimere*, spending five weeks aboard as crew sailing to the islands of Vanuatu. "We were part of the Sailing Medical Ministries Organisation transporting medical supplies to the locals, there being no other way except by boat of reaching the villages," she explained.

That was another adventure for the experienced sailor.

On return to Hastings – one day when she was visiting Rob, he said to her, "Hey, come over here and have a look at this!" He had spotted *Clare* tied up the end of a jetty looking very neglected and abandoned.

"I cried my eyes out when I saw her," she said. "She had no sails on and looked really, really uncared for." She even found a bird's nest in the doghouse. Lanie wanted to buy her back but after much deliberation thought better of it – probably a wise decision, even though *Clare* was on the market at a very cheap price.

Some enquiries revealed that Martin's business had indeed collapsed. No marina fees had been paid for a long time, a huge debt had been incurred and *Clare* was repossessed for the unpaid monies. So, I guess, Martin was in no mood to talk about his time with *Clare*.

What happened to *Clare*? Well, once I'd decided that I'd like to write this story, I had to try and trace past owners to hear their stories. That is not easy. Many enquiries to Border Force (ex-

Customs), Immigration, marinas and State Departments of Transport for records, all drew blanks. No one would reveal any information. It was all very frustrating. Then one day, a light bulb moment occurred!

I was enjoying a coffee at our local Coffee Club when this bloke came and sat at the table in front of me. His back was turned towards me and on his shirt was a big, colourful, Cocos (Keeling) design. I got up and walked over to him, convinced it was John Clunies-Ross.

"Do you mind if I speak to you?" I asked. "Are you John Clunies-Ross from Cocos Islands?"

He laughed, "No, I'm Kim Hughes (ex Australian test captain) but people do mistake me for John! I used to have a property on Cocos. What would you like to know?"

I then explained that I was trying to find out what happened to *Clare* and if he knew Lanie (Helena) Lester, the island nurse back in 1998. He said he knew the story of *Clare* and suggested that I speak to the tourist office on Cocos. I rushed home and flicked off an email, and back came a quick response saying. "Try Helena Verboon – here is a mobile number. "

I sent texts and that was how Lanie and I eventually reconnected after all these years. (Lanie had gone back to using her maiden name).

The final chapter will describe where *Clare* is now, who owns her and the prospects for her future at 70 years of age.

Chapter Six

Wooden boat building in WA

"A sailing vessel is alive in a way that no ship with mechanical power could be,"
                                            Aubrey de Selincourt

A natural reaction, I guess, is that when you become interested in something, many connections begin to link up and you learn lots more about the history of your subject. As mentioned earlier in the book, we became very interested in *Clare's* past and that led us to recognise what an important role the wooden sailing vessel has played in the history of Western Australia. We all understand that our early colonists and settlers arrived on sailing ships and the stories of the *Parmelia, Challenger* and *Sulphur* are well known and taught in our primary schools. The early ancestors of my wife, Aileen, arrived on May 14th 1830 on the *Rockingham*. Unfortunately, the ship ran aground in Cockburn Sound and was wrecked. *Parmelia* also ran aground –the first steps taken ashore by the new settlers were on Garden Island!

What is a little less known was that early sailing masters hated coming to the new colony. After crossing 4,000+ miles of Southern Ocean, they had this island they had to negotiate round (Rottnest) to get into the calmer waters of Gage Roads. The south passage is strewn with reefs so was very hazardous to ships. There was no Rottnest Lighthouse from 1829 until 1851 and that one proved to be inadequate, with only a short range and not enough elevation to see it from quite a way off. Until then, masters had to rely on their navigational skills to find Rottnest, and then pick up a pilot from Fremantle after sailing round the island's northern side to make their way into the fledgling town of Fremantle. There was no river harbour – vessels had to anchor out in the open sea. Eventually, a jetty was built, but it was a very dicey job going alongside with the prevailing SW winds and strong easterlies. A second lighthouse was completed by 1896 – this is still there today. With its 30 metre tower and strong lens, it can propel a beam up to 26nm (nautical miles) these days. However, some vessels still found themselves on the reef and there are 13 wrecks around Rottnest. Masters called the island, 'The Brick on the Landing' because local waters were still very treacherous. A second lighthouse at Bathurst Point improved things: navigators now had two position lines from the lights, and where they intersected gave them a pretty good fix (or position). Pilots were stationed at Rottnest from 1848-1903 (before that they were at Fremantle) and they had to put to sea in all weathers to assist masters. It was a very difficult and scary job. Eventually, with better communications, the pilot service was moved back to Fremantle where it still operates today, handling the largest of ships.

C. Y. O'Connor deserves a mention here. Every child is taught about his famous pipeline to Kalgoorlie for bringing water to the goldfields but less known is that he was behind the design and construction of today's Rottnest Lighthouse, and also for establishing the inner harbour at Fremantle. The early sailing ships could not cross the bar to get upriver – hence having to anchor in the open sea or tie-up to the jetty.

O'Connor came up with a plan to blow up the limestone reef bar, dredge the waters and build the north and south moles. An incredible feat of engineering that made Fremantle a safe, easier harbour to enter – and no doubt, eased the nightmares of captains! The port was officially opened in 1897. It's difficult to believe but in 1897, a record 474 vessels arrived at Fremantle, 127 of them being sailing ships. It has been an important, busy port ever since.

*Fremantle Jetty and wharf area –
before the harbour, it was hazardous for sailing ships*

From the very earliest days of the colony (1829) settlers soon found that local timbers were excellent for boat-building and probably the earliest yard that we know of was established at the Maylands Peninsula, about 190 years ago. That is incredible when you think about it. It's still going strong today and wooden boats are still being restored and built there on the banks of the Swan River.

Swan River Sailing – circa mid 19th century

The importance and need for vessels was recognised early in the piece because of the lack of decent roads and bridges to get goods transported from Fremantle upriver to the new settlements of Perth and Guildford. All kinds of sailing craft were built. Extracts of records I discovered from just 1899 - 1907 show that 300 vessels of varying types were built over eight years. Shipwrights constructed barges, cutters, peter boats (of Dutch design) whaleboats, fishing boats, sailing barges and ferries.

Goods had to be moved upriver and river crossings had to be made with the ferries. Barges were pulled along by sailing boats. Early settlers soon learnt to use the morning easterly breezes and the afternoon 'Fremantle Doctor' to speed up the deliveries. It must have been a delightful sight to see the Swan River so full of sailing boats – unlike the ubiquitous jet-skis and 'stink boats' that pollute the river today. It was not long before cruising yachts and clubs began to make an appearance – Royal Perth Yacht Club was first mooted in 1841 after a regatta. The Club was established in 1865.

An early sailing regatta on the Swan River

Prominading at the Narrows about 1850 – watching the sailing.

Fremantle was also important for wooden boat building and C shed, which was built in 1903 for storage and sorting of cargoes, went on to become a valuable building where repairs and renovations to timber boats were carried out. New vessels were also built there.

Sailing friends, Gene and Vicky, built a beautiful version of Herreshoff's classic ketch *Nereia* in C shed. (Herreshoff was a famous American yacht designer.) They began laying down the keel in 1999 and she was launched about three years later. It cost them a lot of money but she was a real beauty with a clipper bow and lovely lines.

The graceful lines of Atmosphere – *she was built in C shed, Fremantle harbour wharf*

They sailed her round to Queensland where, unfortunately, she had to be sold. She was featured three times in *Cruising Helmsman* magazine, once by me during the building stage (2000), the other two times by Gene as a completed yacht (2003 & 2005).

Atmosphere is easily recognisable and I'm sure she's made many friends plying the Queensland coast.

The most famous wooden sailing ships built in WA in recent times are, of course, the *Endeavour* and *Duyfken* replicas. Both of those beautiful ships are a credit to West Australian shipwrights. Chris Bowman came out from America to help build the *Endeavour*. He originally arrived in Fremantle in 1988 as part of the America's Cup team but stayed on. After the *Endeavour* was launched, he opened a business catering for wooden boats and used C shed on historical Victoria Quay as his premises. It was here that he helped Gene with the construction of *Atmosphere*. C shed today is undergoing refurbishment as a historical building. Lots of asbestos has had to be removed. It'll be an impressive structure and once work is completed, who knows, wooden boats may again be seen there.

The *Endeavour* project was the brainchild of John Longley and was initially financed by Alan Bond and Bond Corporation. The slogan read, 'A Gift to the Nation from Bond Corporation' and was printed on lots of knick-knacks and souvenirs. We still have a beer-drinking mug, now a holder of pens and pencils, with the slogan on it. Bond hit hard times financially and a Japanese consortium took over for a while but they pulled out too. Luckily, with all sorts of support from the community such as private donations, government funding and business company donations, the project was successfully completed and she was launched in 1993. Bondy built a huge shed to house the *Endeavour* at Fremantle Fishing Boat Harbour and the public could go along and watch construction. It was fascinating. Experts would explain and demonstrate traditional methods of building sailing ships so it was all very educational too.

The day of the launching was memorable for all West Australians and thousands went along to watch. We were in the huge crowd. Fred, the old shipwright who fixed that plank on

Clare, was given the honour of cutting the last rope holding the *Endeavour* to the slipway. He swung his axe and she slipped faster and faster down the slope and entered the water with an enormous splash! She bobbed up and floated proudly with thousands of us watching, cheering and clapping. It was all very emotional.

It was some time before her masts were stepped, the interior completed and all the rigging was set up. Myriad other jobs were required to get her seaworthy but when completed, she eventually sailed out of Fremantle harbour on her maiden voyage. We sailed down from Hillarys to Fremantle in *Clare* to participate in the occasion. It was a magic day.

Endeavour under full sail as she sails off around Australia. Clare sailing close by

WA's other famous wooden ship, the *Duyfken*, was built in the grounds of the Western Australian Maritime Museum in Fremantle. Her keel was laid in 1997 and three years later she was launched, rigged and fitted out for sea-trials.

Duyfken under construction at Fremantle – beautiful wood working

Again, a team of local designers, researchers, shipwrights, riggers, blacksmiths, sail makers and wood carvers were assembled for the project. There was a lot of communication with the Dutch too – helping with the plans and other advice. Like the *Endeavour*, the *Duyfken* proved to be a safe, seaworthy vessel. She was fast and easy to manoeuvre, just like her 16th-century prototype.

Maintaining these wooden ships was very expensive. Both are loved by West Australians but the only real solution to ensure their longevity was to have them moored in Sydney at the National Maritime Museum where they lie today. Visitors can still climb aboard and explore these lovely ships and even go for sails on Sydney Harbour.

The lovely Duyfken under full sail in local waters

Perhaps you've noticed a 'theme' going through this book? Yes – you're quite right. Wooden vessels do take lots of time and money to maintain and many hearts have been broken along the way, including bank accounts! But I have to add that *Clare* gave us far more pleasure than grief. She was a fine ketch to sail and undoubtedly was our favourite.

Another very fine wooden boat builder from WA was Arthur Bishop, as mentioned earlier. He mainly seemed to build yachts in the 30-foot range but one of his biggest yachts was the 1951-built *Gelasma*. She was 42 feet long with a narrow beam and was raced for many years on the Swan River. As mentioned, along with *Clare* and *Vivian of Straun*, she was a big yacht for river racing. *Brigadoon* was another lovely example of Arthur's work and skills. She is a motor-sailer, very comfortable, with a big doghouse and was used for charter. His yachts are still around and are loved and sailed by proud owners. He began his business in Claremont and eventually moved to East Fremantle. Arthur has several boats listed in the National Maritime Historical Registration. I actually met him at a nursing home in Mandurah shortly before he died. He was still very aware in his 90s and I was able to tell him how much I admired his yachts. He seemed pleased that someone knew who he was. He was still adamant that *Clare* was not designed or built by him!

The Amateur Boat Builder's Association (ABBA) is an ongoing group that meets at the South of Perth Yacht Club. This group of enthusiasts work in all types of material: timber, aluminium, steel and other methods. About half the members have projects underway - ranging from dinghies to ocean-going yachts and historic rebuilds. Other members have completed boats or are restoring classics like *Clare* or just have an interest in all things nautical.

A beautiful example of wooden boat building from the ABBA

Another contemporary boat-builder in WA is Tony O'Connor. Tony is building some lovely boats at East Rockingham, and 2021 marks his 25th year as a boat builder. He first got into the trade in the 1980s and his main interest was in traditional boat building, particularly clinker planking. His first paying job, after qualifying, was to build a 24-foot replica of a

Thames rowing skiff. Tony says he can't remember the exact figure but building it involved several thousand small copper nails and an equal amount of even tinier copper roves, which are like washers.

Over the years he built and repaired many traditional clinker boats and he has admitted that counting nails became a familiar exercise, along with wondering if there was possibly an easier way of fastening all those nails? Nowadays almost all of the clinker planking he does is epoxy glued – so he supposes that modern technology has provided an answer for, or at least an alternative, to nails. Epoxy glued clinker is much easier and faster, and for amateurs much more forgiving than traditional clinker. The only drawback is cleaning up excess glue, which he finds is best done as soon as possible before the glue has set.

"Whilst traditionally built boats may be pleasant to work on, the fact is that the majority of work for a boat-builder these days involves a wide range of building techniques, both traditional and modern, and I have found over the years that the variety of work I do is probably the thing I like most about my job," says Tony.

So he finds that within a short space of time he can go from traditional planking repairs to interior fitting out, and then to composite construction and/or repair.

Being a boat-builder does involve working on boats that aren't made of wood. "I work on fibreglass and aluminium boats too. These boats have plenty of wooden parts, usually, and the better quality boats can have some very fine quality woodwork in them which I find very satisfying to work on," he added.

One of the prettiest little yachts Tony has completed is the Vivier gaff yawl *Jewel*. As you can see from the picture, this is a lovely design.

*The gaff-rigged 'Jewel' sailing on Cockburn Sound.
More wonderful boat building in the 21st century*

Francois Vivier lives in Pornichet, France and enjoys an international reputation as a naval architect and designer. Tony is also licenced to build other Vivier designs and is also a supplier of CNC kits (a bit like a boat-in-a-box), kits which he can build, or help new owners to construct.

So the traditions of wooden boat building are alive and well in Western Australia and the skills needed to bring these vessels to life will continue.

Chapter Seven

Brad's Story and *Clare* Today

"If you find a really happy man, you will find him building a wooden boat,"

David Wolfe

Lanie met Brad Raynor after she saw *Clare* out on the hard in Hastings, Victoria, and approached him about the boat. She contacted me with his details and I was able to put together *Clare's* current whereabouts and get to know her present owner – a very genuine bloke.

Here's Brad's story:

Brad's been interested in wooden boats since he began his apprenticeship at sixteen. He's always loved timber and working with it. He bought his first wooden boat in Manly, Queensland, when he was in his 30s. It was a beautiful old yacht called *Ellida* that was built back in the 1940s. She had sailed in a couple of Sydney to Hobart races. Brad spent about two years working on her, restoring her and then sailed away to the Whitsundays and up and down the east coast. That's when he fell in love with wooden boats.

Ellida was a sloop-rigged 33-footer and was a double-ender, a

Carmen design. Carmen's morphed into Swanson yachts – famous double-enders very popular with cruisers. *Ellida's* construction was started before the war and ended up being completed in Manly, Sydney. It was easy for Brad to restore her as he could do everything himself. It was not a stressful project for him. Brad owns a 21-foot trailer-sailer too – a little fibreglass yacht – but says there is a distinct difference between a timber yacht and a plastic one. We can vouch for that as well.

Regarding *Clare*, he says he and his kids sort of, "fell upon her" looking very neglected.

Brad's son dreams of sailing off to tropical Pacific Islands!

He thought she could be ideal for his dream of sailing out to the Pacific Islands. He said one bloke who wanted to buy her was going to transport her into the bush and bury her to live on! That was, of course, totally impractical as the timbers would eventually rot. Brad says he was glad he got onto *Clare* before this happened. Other 'solutions' for *Clare* were to cut her up for the wood (there is pristine jarrah under all that paint) and sell off all the parts. By this time, the marina owners were becoming desperate wondering what to do with her as she was taking up space with no revenue coming in.

So Brad put in an offer and it was accepted. He could not let her be destroyed just for the wood.

Brad looks very determined to complete a high quality restoration on Clare.

*2021 – Clare is 70 years old
but that jarrah is still pristine under the paintwork*

He finds it a very rewarding and enjoyable experience working on *Clare*. Brad admits that he finds it exciting replacing damaged ribs, using good timbers.

Brad begins to replace cracked ribs – a huge job

His first job was to gut the insides, taking out all the old furniture, thus being able to get at the bare hull for the repairs. He found the concrete ballast in the bilge had to be jackhammered out, as he wasn't sure of the wood underneath. But all is ok and the keel is sound. There is some surface rot due to freshwater getting into the bilge but overall no real dramas. Brad didn't want to spend too much on her until he was sure all the timbers were ok. The hull planking is still pristine underneath the paint and that was a huge relief.

One thing he found in the bilge were iron balls (for extra ballast) – anything steel can cause rot in timber.

Brad found some rot in the timbers and was surprised that Clare had not foundered at some point.

These have been removed. Most of the ribs on both sides of the boat are broken in two or three places and these will have to be replaced. For these, he'll use a combination of jarrah and merbu (a timber similar in character to jarrah).

Brad says he's excited with the progress and would prefer to be working on *Clare* full-time but he's very busy with his 'day job'. He's also bringing up two teenagers on his own – nice kids but they do have their moments. They are looking forward to sailing the Pacific with dad. He's also renovating a house, so all that keeps him really busy and he just fits in *Clare* when he can.

Brad has completed replacing the ribs on the starboard side. Wonderful work with a mix of jarrah and merbu timbers'

More interior work nears completion. it's a big job but the end result will be well worth it.

Brad says he is delighted that he has a beautiful project ahead of him, despite what some of the so-called 'experts' say and who advise him on the best way to tackle the work. He knows what he's doing. 'Armchair' experts abound when you own a wooden boat – it's almost as if they come out of the woodwork!

"It's going to come together for me, all the planking is in good order and the keel's in good order so I'm on a winner there," he explained to me over the phone.

"Two timbers - merbu and jarrah (similar in characteristics and colour) will be used to replace the ribs," he explained. As for the furniture, Brad says he'll redesign that to make it more suitable for taking on extra crew. He has kept what's salvageable of the furniture but so much of it was broken, or rotten, that it's not really viable to put it back. Over the years, many people have added things so redoing it all from scratch makes a lot of sense. He added, "You never know who might want to come sailing – or I might just be on my own!"

Where the mast steps onto the keelson, there's a lot of rot because of the steel mast support. That will have to be replaced by laminated timber as it bears the whole weight of the rig. He found quite a bit of steel in the boat – that causes a reaction with wood so has to be removed.

He continued, "She'll be perfect when she's finished. My vision was always to buy a yacht of that size, maybe spend $150,00 on a boat – then another $50,000 getting it up to scratch and up to my standard. So I've decided to put that money into *Clare* instead and she'll give me everything I need. She's done it for 70 years and I reckon she can do it for another 70 years!"

I added that I thought *Clare* was a great seaboat that sails well. With her ketch-cutter rig, she goes well to windward and is comfortable off the wind.

It may take Brad two or three years to complete the project as he's not in a rush and can take his time. He has the skill sets to make this a really worthwhile project and the completed project will be a wonderful addition to the Australian Register of Historic Vessels. She is already a registered Australian ship bearing the official number 854838, as we had to register her to sail overseas.

Aileen, Lanie and I are all looking forward to seeing *Clare* back in the water and we hope to be part of Brad's crew on his first sail.

Epilogue

I do hope you've enjoyed our voyage with *Clare* and the other wooden sailing vessels I've mentioned. The sailing vessel is tied up with the whole history of Western Civilisation, exploration, colonisation (and often exploitation) and recreation.

Lanie is back home in Leongatha, Victoria, working as the community's midwife. Leongatha is a very pleasant dairy farming town set among rolling hills. She still dreams of sailing – and does, on occasions, on friends' yachts. She is making plans to caravan around Australia.

Brad is working slowly and thoroughly through the restoration of *Clare* and dreaming of the day he can sail away to his Pacific Islands.

We don't own a yacht now we're fully retired. It's too expensive, what with pen fees, club fees and maintenance. We still do take an occasional sail with friends. Aileen and I feel very proud to have owned, sailed and lived on two lovely wooden boats.

Nigel Ridgway,
Gwelup, WA
January, 2021

Great Sailing Reads!

- 1606 - an Epic Adventure, Evan McHugh
- A World on My Own, Robin Knox-Johnston
- Adrift. Steven, Callahan
- Close to the Wind, Peter Goss
- Dave the Brave, Cyril Ayris
- Desperate Voyage, John Caldwell
- Dolphins at Sunset, Elizabeth Thurston
- Fatal Storm, Rob Mundle
- First Lady, Kay Cottee
- Gipsy Moth Circles the World, Francis Chichester
- Knockdown, Martin Dugard
- Lionheart, Jesse Martin
- Maiden Voyage, Tania Aebi
- Once is Enough, Miles Smeeton
- Sailing Alone Around the World, Joshua Slocum
- Sextant, Sea and Solitude. Hugh Schmitt
- South Sea Vagabonds, John Wray
- Still Cruising, Lisa Copeland
- Storm Tactics, Lin and Larry Pardey
- The Dove, Robin Lee-Graham
- The Incredible Voyage, Tristan Jones
- The Long Way, Bernard Moitessier
- The Riddle of the Sands, Erskine Childers
- The Strange Voyage of Donald Crowhurst, Nicholas Tomalin
- Turkey Spam on Sunday, Marilyn Morgan

By the same author:

Lotus 11, an Indian Ocean Adventure – Access Press (1992)

A Different Drummer - the escapades of a ten-pound Pom – Linellen Press (2020)

About the Author

Nigel was born in Somerset, UK, and was a child of Her Majesty's services; moving around England, Germany and Jordan. He attended two boarding schools. His early working life was mainly as an unskilled worker, trying many jobs. He emigrated to Australia in 1966 as a 'Ten Pound Pom,' arriving in WA after working in Queensland.

Nigel eventually became a West Australian primary teacher for twenty-one years, then a high school relief teacher, while all his adult life he also played music part-time.

He married a 4th generation West Australian lady, Aileen, in 1991. They are very happy. Nigel has always sailed since high school in Germany, and has had many adventures, both overseas and around the coast of Australia.

He still plays music with Perth's *New Orleans Heritage Jazzband* and the cabaret band *Haze*. Since retiring he has become a Rottnest Guide, and an active member of U3A (University of the Third Age). He's always had a passion for writing and wrote, *Lotus 11 – an Indian Ocean Adventure* (1992) and a 'sortamemoir' *A Different Drummer* (2020). He wrote for *'Cruising Helmsman'* magazine for over twenty years (1990-2012). He is a popular guest speaker for U3A and Probus. Nigel has a Diploma in Nautical Science and is a Yachtmaster (Ocean).

www.ingramcontent.com/pod-product-compliance
Lightning Source LLC
Chambersburg PA
CBHW041957080526
44588CB00021B/2782